Harold R Foster

Prince Valiant

COMPRISING PAGES 1597 THROUGH 1640

The Dead Warrior's Sword

FANTAGRAPHICS BOOKS

ABOUT THIS EDITION:

Produced in cooperation with the Danish publisher Carlsen and several other publishers around the world, this new edition of PRINCE VALIANT is intended to be the definitive compilation of Hal Foster's masterpiece.

In addition to this volume, Fantagraphics Books has in stock thirty-two more collections of Foster's Prince Valiant work (Vols. 1-2 and 6-35). The ultimate goal is to have the entirety of Hal Foster's epic, comprising 40 volumes, in print at once.

ABOUT THE PUBLISHER:

FANTAGRAPHICS BOOKS has dedicated itself to bringing readers the finest in comic book and comic strip material, both new and old. Its "classics" division includes *The Complete E.C. Segar Popeye*, the *Complete Little Nemo in Slumberland* hardcover collection, and *Pogo* and *Little Orphan Annie* reprints. Its "modern" division is responsible for such works as *Love and Rockets* by Los Bros. Hernandez, Peter Bagge's *Hate*, Daniel Clowes's *Eightball*, Chris Ware's *ACME*, and American editions of work by Muñoz & Sampayo, Lewis Trondheim, and F. Solano Lopez, as well as *The Complete Crumb Comics*.

PREVIOUS VOLUMES IN THIS SERIES:

PRINCE VALIANT, Volume 36
"The Dead Warrior's Sword"
comprising pages 1597 (September 17, 1967) through 1640 (July 14, 1968)
Published by Fantagraphics Books, 7563 Lake City Way NE, Seattle, WA 98115
Editorial Co-Ordinator: Henning Kure and Jens Trasborg
Colored by Jesper Ejsing
Cover inked by Mardøn Smet
Fantagraphics Books staff: Kim Thompson and Mark Vick
Copyright ©1999 King Features Syndicate, Inc., Bull's, Interpresse, & Fantagraphics Books, Inc.
Printed in Denmark
ISBN 1-56097-348-X
First Printing: Spring, 1999

Our Story: NOEL REACHES SIR GRENWOLD AT DAWN AND HE RECOGNIZES THE HALF-BURNED PARCHMENT AS THE WILL HE WITNESSED AND AGREES TO RIDE TO WICKWAIN AND STRAIGHTEN OUT THE DISPUTED INHERITANCE.

ON THE WAY THEY MEET PRINCE VALIANT BINDING UP A WOUND. HE HAS APPARENTLY BEEN WORKING LATE THAT NIGHT, FOR THE ASSASSINS WHO HAD BEEN SENT TO STOP NOEL ARE LYING IN RESTFUL POSES ON THE GRASS.

THE GATES OF WICKWAIN ARE CLOSED, BUT ON A TERRACE, BALA, HIS BACK TO THE WALL, IS STRIVING MIGHTILY TO HOLD OFF SLIGOL'S MEN. *"COME, I KNOW A SECRET WAY INTO THE CASTLE!"* SHOUTS NOEL.

THEY FOLLOW NOEL DOWN THE CLIFF TO THE BASE OF THE WALLS WHERE A WOODEN DOOR, PAINTED TO RESEMBLE THE ROCK, OPENS ON A DARK PASSAGE.

FROM A SAFE POSITION IN THE REAR SLIGOL HAS BEEN URGING HIS MEN TO THE ATTACK, BUT NOW, AS VAL, GRENWOLD AND NOEL STORM UP THE STAIR HE FINDS HIMSELF IN THE FOREFRONT. SWORDS FLASH IN THE SUNLIGHT AND SLIGOL LOSES ALL INTEREST IN OWNING WICKWAIN.

GRIM-FACED BALA AND WILD-EYED MEG ARE STILL HOLDING OUT AS THE THREE KNIGHTS HACK THEIR WAY TO THE TERRACE.
SLIGOL'S GUARDS, NEVER TOO ENTHUSIASTIC, ARE GLAD TO LAY DOWN THEIR ARMS.

1597   9-17

FONDE IS FOUND COWERING IN THE KITCHEN AND MEG, WITH HER CRIMSONED SPEAR, HAS TO BE RESTRAINED. THE GATES ARE OPENED AND FONDE IS LAST SEEN RUNNING TOWARD THE SAFETY OF THE FOREST.
NEXT WEEK— **The Hero**

Prince Valiant
IN THE DAYS OF KING ARTHUR
BY Harold R Foster

Our Story: SLIGOL DIES OF A STROKE, LEAVING HIS WARRIORS WITHOUT A LEADER. ALTHOUGH THEY ADMIRE THE SKILL WITH WHICH PRINCE VALIANT AND HIS FRIENDS HANDLE THEIR BRIGHT SWORDS, THEY DO NOT WISH FURTHER DEMONSTRATIONS. THEY THROW DOWN THEIR WEAPONS.

VAL TURNS TO BALA: "WELL DONE, BALA. YOU RISKED YOUR LIFE, LIKE A TRUE KNIGHT, TO HOLD THE CASTLE UNTIL WE ARRIVED. KING ARTHUR SHALL HEAR OF THIS."
THEN HE SEEKS THE CHAMBER OF LADY CLIVE TO ASSURE HER THAT ALL THE LEGAL CLAIMS HAVE BEEN SETTLED IN A SATISFACTORY MANNER AND WICKWAIN BELONGS TO HER.

BALA IS NOT USED TO COMPLIMENTS, AND PRAISE FROM SUCH A FAMOUS KNIGHT AS SIR VALIANT GOES TO HIS HEAD. "THANK YOU FOR YOUR HELP, MEG," HE SAYS IN A LOFTY MANNER, "BUT I COULD HAVE HANDLED THE MATTER ALONE."

"I WAS NOT HELPING YOU," SNAPS MEG, "I WAS PROTECTING MYSELF--- AND I CAN DO THAT WITHOUT YOUR HELP!"
BALA LOOKS AT HER WITH NEW INTEREST; THE STOCKY FIGURE, SNUB NOSE, RED HAIR, AND THE ANGRY GLINT IN HER BLUE EYES. PERHAPS SHE IS RIGHT!

BALA THINKS OF LADY ANN, SO NEARLY HIS...HER PRETTY FACE, SMALL FEET AND HANDS.. SO HELPLESS, NOT AT ALL LIKE MEG.

HE WATCHES MEG, FASCINATED, AS SHE PUTS THE PRISONERS TO WORK CLEANING UP THE MESS. SHE IS A HEALTHY YOUNG THING, HE SPECULATES, QUITE COMPETENT, AND WOULD MAKE A GOOD WIFE FOR A WARRIOR. BUT THEN, WHO WANTS A WIFE? NOT HE!
NEXT WEEK—YES—he!

1598   9-24

Our Story: BALA WHISTLES MERRILY AS HE POLISHES HIS ARMOR AND PUTS AN EDGE ON HIS SWORD, FOR HAS NOT SIR VALIANT PAID HIM A COMPLIMENT AND GIVEN HIM CREDIT FOR HOLDING THE CASTLE?

THE EFFICIENT MEG CALLS IN THE SURVIVORS OF SLIGOL'S TROOP, HIRES THE BEST AND SENDS THE REST ON THEIR WAY.

WHILE VAL, AS THE KING'S DEPUTY, SIGNS A TITLE TO WICKWAIN AS CLOSE TO THE LATE EARL CLIVE'S WILL AS THEY CAN REMEMBER. NOW, THE MISSION COMPLETE, THEY WILL RETURN TO CAMELOT NEXT DAY.

MOVED BY A PLEASANT RESTLESSNESS BALA WANDERS TO THE TERRACE WHERE HE AND MEG FOUGHT SLIGOL'S WARRIORS. TO HIS SURPRISE MEG IS THERE, BUT SHE LOOKS DIFFERENT. HER HAIR IS REARRANGED AND SHE WEARS A MORE BECOMING GOWN.

"WE RETURN TO CAMELOT ON THE MORROW AND I WAS WONDERING, PERHAPS, IF MAYBE I HAPPENED TO RIDE THIS WAY AGAIN, WOULD I BE WELCOME?"
MEG CONSIDERS: "HE IS A BIT STUPID, HIS MANNERS ARE CRUDE, BUT HE IS STRONG AND HEALTHY AND I AM SURE I CAN MAKE SOME IMPROVEMENTS IN HIM."

"IF SUCH AN IMPROBABLE THING SHOULD HAPPEN I AM SURE MOTHER WOULD WELCOME YOU." THEN SHE SEES THE ADORING LOOK IN HIS EYES AND ADDS: "I WOULD BE PLEASED, TOO."

ON THE WAY TO WICKWAIN BALA HAD BEEN A SULLEN, SILENT COMPANION AND VAL HAD IGNORED HIM. BUT NOW HE IS FULL OF SONG AND JEST AND THESE SYMPTOMS ARE ALL TOO FAMILIAR.
"IS IT THAT LITTLE REDHEAD?" VAL ASKS. "YES!" ANSWERS THE BEMUSED BALA, "THE FAIREST MAID ON THIS WONDERFUL EARTH!"   NEXT WEEK — The Hunt

Our Story: AS THEY RIDE TO CAMELOT BALA AND PRINCE VALIANT ARE BUFFETED BY A WIND AND RAINSTORM THAT STRIP THE LAST OF THE AUTUMN LEAVES FROM THE TREES. VAL IS ELATED, FOR WITH THE LEAVES DOWN, THE HUNTING SEASON BEGINS.

THERE ARE OTHER SIGNS. ALETA HAS DESIGNED A NEW COSTUME FOR THE HUNT, AND PRINCE ARN IS OUT IN THE YARD PRACTICING WITH BOW AND SPEAR.

AFTER VAL HAS MADE HIS REPORT, ARTHUR LOOKS UP FROM THE BOAR SPEAR HE IS SHARPENING AND SAYS: "*I KNEW YOU WOULD FULFILL YOUR MISSION. NOW, IF WE HAVE A SHARP FROST TONIGHT WE BEGIN THE HUNT ON THE MORROW.*"

THE KING AND KNIGHTS DINE MERRILY. THAT IS, ALL BUT THE ROYAL HUNTSMAN. TO HIM FALLS THE RESPONSIBILITY OF GUIDING THE HUNTERS TO THE BEST PLACES, TO ARRANGE OVERNIGHT SHELTER, STABLING OF HORSES, AND KENNELS FOR THE HOUNDS. THE GAME THAT FALLS TO THE HUNTERS IS DIVIDED ACCORDING TO LAW.

THE HUNT IS MORE THAN SPORT, IT IS A HARVEST. FOR THE KING HAS MANY RETAINERS AND GUESTS TO FEED. FOLLOWING THE HUNTERS COME THE BUTCHERS, SERVANTS, BEATERS, AND OXCARTS TO CARRY THE VENISON TO SMOKEHOUSES AND SALTING VATS.

DAY AWAKES TO THE SOUND OF HORNS, AND WITH SONGS AND LAUGHTER THE HUNTING PARTY WENDS ITS WAY ACROSS THE FROSTY MEADOWS AND ENTERS THE DIM PARKLANDS.

NEXT WEEK— **Hunted Hunters**

1600 10-8

Our Story: THE FIRST DAY'S HUNT IS A SUCCESS AND MANY AN OXCART LOADED WITH VENISON TRUNDLES BACK TO CAMELOT.

SOME CARTS HOLD MORE THAN VENISON. FOR INSTANCE, THERE IS SIR DUMBOLD WHO WAS CLUMSY WITH HIS BOAR SPEAR AND GOT SLASHED BY THE ANIMAL'S TUSKS.

ARGOTH, OVERCONFIDENT OF HIS OWN STRENGTH, MISJUDGED THE POWER OF A WOUNDED STAG.....

.......ALSO SHIPPED HOME BY CART IS SIR TRAWLEY. HE PAID THE PRICE OF GIRL-WATCHING WHEN HE SHOULD HAVE KEPT HIS EYES AHEAD.

EVER IN THE FOREFRONT RIDES KING ARTHUR, HIS FACE AGLOW WITH THE EXCITEMENT OF THE HUNT. ALL TOO SELDOM CAN HE PUT ASIDE THE CARES OF STATE.

THE HUNT GOES MERRILY ON. ONLY THE MASTER OF THE HOUNDS SUFFERS. FOR TO HIM IT SEEMS THAT IT IS ALWAYS THE BRAVEST AND BEST THAT FALL TO TUSK AND HORN.

THE PARTY RESTS FOR THE NIGHT AT PONSBY CASTLE, AND THOUGH THEIR HOST IS FLATTERED TO ENTERTAIN HIS KING, HE KNOWS HE WILL NOW FACE THE WINTER WITH EMPTY WINE CELLAR AND BARE LARDER.

NEXT WEEK— *Aleta becomes Diana*

Our Story: THE SECOND DAY OF THE HUNT DAWNS IN MIST AND RAIN, AND ALETA UNHAPPILY PACKS HER RIDING COSTUME IN THE SADDLEBAG AND DONS A MORE SERVICEABLE CLOAK AND SKIRT.

MOST OF THE LADIES STAY IN THE SHELTER OF THE CASTLE, BUT NOT ALETA. SHE HAS COME TO HUNT AND INTENDS TO ENJOY EVERY MINUTE OF IT, NO MATTER HOW MISERABLE SHE FEELS.

A STAG IS BROUGHT TO BAY AND, AS ALETA STRINGS HER BOW FOR THE KILL, THE HUNTERS MOVE BACK. FOR WELL THEY REMEMBER LAST YEAR'S HUNT WHEN SHE BAGGED THE EARL OF DIREGARDE.

THE STAG IS UNWILLING TO DIE EVEN AT SO FAIR A HAND...... HE CHARGES. FOR A BREATHLESS MOMENT IT LOOKS AS IF HE HAS GORED AND CARRIED AWAY THE DAINTY HUNTRESS.

THE KING IS FIRST TO RECOVER FROM THE SURPRISE. "LOOK!" HE SHOUTS, "THERE GOES THE BEST-DRESSED STAG IN OUR FOREST!" AND BEFORE THE HUNTSMEN REALIZE WHAT HAS HAPPENED HE HAS COVERED ALETA WITH HIS CLOAK.

THE CLOAK IS TOO SHORT, THE WIND IS COLD, AND SHE WOULD DEARLY LOVE TO SLAP THAT SILLY GRIN OFF VAL'S FACE!

PRINCE ARN HAS STRAYED AND IS LISTENING FOR THE BAYING OF THE HOUNDS TO LEAD HIM BACK TO THE PARTY. BUT HIS PRESENCE HAS DISTURBED A HUGE BOAR AND IT IS PLAIN THAT SOMEONE IS GOING TO BE HURT.

NEXT WEEK—The Madman

1602   10-22

Our Story: PRINCE ARN REINS IN HIS HORSE. HIS WAY IS BEING DISPUTED BY A HUGE BOAR WHOSE BLAZING EYES MAKE IT PLAIN THAT SOMEONE IS GOING TO BE HURT.

ARN DISMOUNTS AND READIES HIS SPEAR, BUTT TO GROUND, AND AWAITS THE CHARGE.

THE CHARGE COMES IN A BURST OF FURY, NOT AT ARN BUT TOWARD HIS MOUNT, WHO, SENSING THE DANGER, FLEES IN TERROR. THE TWO VANISH INTO THE FOREST.

NOW HE MUST GET RID OF THE BOAR BEFORE HE CAN CALL IN HIS FRIGHTENED HORSE. A RUSTLING IN THE UNDERBRUSH ATTRACTS HIS ATTENTION. HE ADVANCES CAUTIOUSLY, BUT THE CRACKLING OF TWIGS KEEPS AHEAD OF HIM LEADING HIM ON.

THE BOAR IS THE MOST DANGEROUS ANIMAL IN THE FOREST, AND ARN'S EVERY SENSE IS ALERT TO DANGER. JUST IN TIME HE SEES A WILD-LOOKING FIGURE IN THE BRANCHES, ABOUT TO SPRING. ARN SETS HIS SPEAR AND WITH A FRIGHTENED SCREAM THE WILD MAN SCRAMBLES BACK ON THE LIMB.

THE WILD MAN IS NOT ALONE. A HAG RISES FROM THE UNDERBRUSH, CACKLING: "WE NEARLY HAD YOU THAT TIME, PRETTY BOY, AND ALL YOUR FINE THINGS WOULD BE OURS."
THE CREATURE DROPS TO THE GROUND, ALL HIS FEROCITY GONE. HE BEGINS TO WHIMPER.

THE HAG COMFORTS HIM: "THERE, THERE, BABY, COME INTO THE CAVE AND MOTHER WILL GIVE YOU YOUR MEDICINE AND MAKE YOU WELL AGAIN."

NEXT WEEK—Pretty Things

1603

10-29

Our Story: THE HAG LEADS HER DEMENTED SON AWAY, THEN SHE TURNS: "COME, PRETTY BOY, WE WILL GIVE YOU FOOD AND DRINK. YOU DID NOT HARM US, WE WILL NOT HARM YOU."

THEIR CAVE IS FILTHY, BUT THE WATER IS PURE AND THE STOCKPOT YIELDS UP A FRAGRANT STEW.
"COME, BABY, TAKE YOUR MEDICINE," CACKLES THE HAG, "THEN GO OUT AND FIND MOTHER SOME PRETTIES. THE HUNT IS OUR HARVEST TIME."

THE WILDMAN DRAINS THE CUP. FOR A LONG WHILE HE SITS QUIETLY, THEN HIS FACE CHANGES, A WILD LIGHT SHINES IN HIS EYES. HE GLARES AT ARN WITH SUCH AN EXPRESSION OF HATE THAT ARN READIES SPEAR AND HUNTING KNIFE.

"THERE HE GOES. HE'S SUCH A GOOD BABY AND BRINGS HIS MOTHER LOTS OF PRETTIES. LOOK!" A CLOSET IS OVERFLOWING WITH LOOT. THE RICH MANTLE OF A MERCHANT NEXT TO THE PATCHED AND THREADBARE CLOAK OF A PEASANT, WORN SHOES, BELTS, KNIVES AND TUNICS. THE BLOODSTAINS GIVE EVIDENCE OF HOW THEY WERE OBTAINED.

"AND WHAT WAS THE MEDICINE YOU GAVE YOUR SON?" ASKS ARN. "A BREW I LEARNED FROM MY MAN. HE WAS SKALD ON A VIKING RAIDER AND MADE IT FROM A SECRET MUSHROOM. IT WAS GIVEN TO THE WARRIORS TO DRIVE THEM FIGHTING MAD. THEY BECAME BERSERKERS, ONES WHO NEVER QUIT A FIGHT EXCEPT AS VICTORS."

AT DUSK BABY RETURNS CARRYING ONE OF THE KING'S DEERHOUNDS AND A CLOAK, BELT AND SPEAR THAT ARN RECOGNIZES AS BELONGING TO ONE OF THE BEATERS. ALL ARE BLOODSTAINED.

THERE IS A RUBY IN THE HILT OF ARN'S KNIFE. HE STICKS IT IN THE GROUND WHERE THE FIRELIGHT WILL SHINE ON IT.
"PLAN NO TREACHERY IN THE NIGHT FOR I HAVE SET THE MAGIC RED EYE TO WATCH YOU." THEN HE GOES PEACEFULLY TO SLEEP.

BUT HIS PARENTS GET NO SLEEP, FOR HIS HORSE COMES BACK WITHOUT ITS RIDER. FIRST A DEERHOUND IS MISSING, THEN A SERVANT, AND NOW ARN.

NEXT WEEK — The Berserker

Our Story: BABY IS EXHAUSTED. HE HAS HAD A HARD DAY AND AN OVERDOSE OF 'MEDICINE'. HE IS IN A COMA. BUT THE HAG HAS OTHER PLANS. PRINCE ARN IS STRONG AND HEALTHY, SO SHE DOCTORS HIS STEW WITH THE MEDICINE.

AT FIRST HE IS DIZZY AND A LITTLE SICK, BUT IT PASSES AND STRENGTH RETURNS, A STRENGTH HE HAS NEVER KNOWN. HE WANTS TO RUN, TO WRESTLE. HE HEARS THE HAG'S VOICE SAYING, "GO GATHER PRETTIES. YOU HATE THE HUNTERS. GO TAKE THEIR PRETTIES!"

HE STANDS UP, THE LIGHT OF MADNESS IN HIS EYES. "YOU FILTHY CARRION!" HE HISSES. "NO, NO!" SHE SCREAMS, "HATE THE HUNTERS. TAKE THEIR PRETTIES. WE ARE YOUR FRIENDS!"

VAL AND ALETA SCOUR THE FOREST IN SEARCH OF ARN. AT LAST THEY FIND HIM WANDERING, DAZED AND BLEEDING FROM A WOUND IN HIS SIDE.

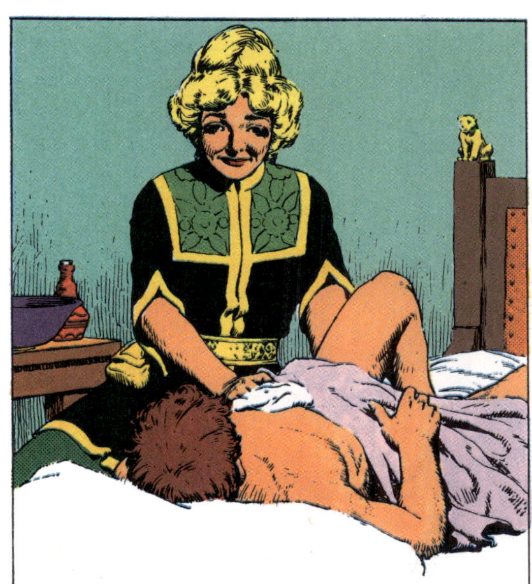

ALETA TAKES HIM BACK AND DRESSES HIS WOUND. IT IS A RELIEF TO KNOW THAT NONE OF THE HUNTERS HAS BEEN MISSING WHILE ARN WAS UNDER THE INFLUENCE OF THE DRUG.

WITH THE HELP OF THE HOUNDS VAL AT LAST FINDS THE HOVEL. ONE GLANCE AND THE STORY IS PLAIN, AND THE CLOSET IN WHICH THE HAG HAD KEPT HER 'PRETTIES' REVEALS THE NUMBER OF MURDERS HER BABY HAS COMMITTED.

1605　© King Features Syndicate, Inc. 1967. World rights reserved.　11-12

VAL STACKS DRY WOOD BOTH INSIDE AND OUT AND SETS IT AFLAME. AN EVIL NEST IS PURIFIED BY FLAME.

NEXT WEEK — **Return to Duty**

Our Story: THE GREAT HUNT COMES TO AN END. THE HARVEST HAS BEEN A GOOD ONE AND THERE WILL BE MEAT FOR ALL THROUGH THE COMING WINTER. THE ROYAL HUNTSMAN WORKS ALL NIGHT TO SEE THAT EACH VILLAGE, EACH HOST GETS A FAIR SHARE.

THREE WONDERFUL WEEKS KING ARTHUR HAS HAD, FAR FROM THE CARES OF STATE. IT IS A SMALL PARTY THAT TAKES THE LONG ROAD BACK TO CAMELOT, FOR ONLY THE KEENEST HUNTERS HAVE STAYED TO THE END. IT IS A MERRY GROUP, BUT AS THEY NEAR HOME THE KING FALLS SILENT, WONDERING WHAT PROBLEMS AWAIT HIM.

HE HAS NOT LONG TO WAIT. HARDLY HAVE THEY DISMOUNTED THAN MORDRED COMES ROARING: "MY BROTHER GAWAIN IS HELD PRISONER BY BALDA HAN IN THE LAND OF DATHRAM. A SLAVE, HELD FOR RANSOM!"

"I DEMAND A FLEET OF SHIPS AND AN ARMY FOR HIS RESCUE. YOU ARE HIS UNCLE, IT IS YOUR DUTY. I WILL BE IN COMMAND AND TAKE FULL VENGEANCE ON BALDA HAN FOR THIS CRIME!"

THE MESSENGER WHO BROUGHT THE RANSOM LETTER IS SUMMONED. "YES, IT IS TRUE, I WAS WITH SIR GAWAIN IN THE SLAVE PENS, BUT WAS RELEASED TO CARRY THIS LETTER. HE WAS ALIVE THEN, BUT THAT WAS MONTHS AGO, AND SLAVES OF BALDA HAN DO NOT LIVE LONG."

"SIR VALIANT, IN YOUR ADVENTURING DID YOU EVER VISIT THE LAND OF DATHRAM?" ASKS THE KING.
"YES, SIRE, IT HAS A FORTIFIED SEAPORT FROM WHICH CORSAIRS SCOUR THE SEA FOR PLUNDER AND SLAVES."

1606   © King Features Syndicate, Inc., 1967. World rights reserved.   11-19

"BUT BALDA HAN'S CITY IS IN THE HILLS OF DAG, BEYOND A BURNING DESERT THAT HAS SWALLOWED ARMIES. ONLY HIS CARAVAN DRIVERS KNOW THE BITTER WAY ACROSS."

NEXT WEEK—The Long Journey

Our Story: MORDRED DEMANDS SHIPS AND MEN BE ASSIGNED TO HIM IMMEDIATELY TO RESCUE HIS HALF-BROTHER, SIR GAWAIN, FROM THE HANDS OF BALDA HAN. BUT THE KING WAVES HIM AWAY AND SITS LONG IN THOUGHT.

PRINCE VALIANT LEAVES ARTHUR WITH HIS WORRIES AND WALKS HOME TO FIND SOME OF HIS OWN. ALETA IS ONCE MORE THE QUEEN AND BEFORE HER SIT THE ENVOYS FROM HER KINGDOM IN THE MISTY ISLES, BRINGING THEIR ANNUAL REPORT. AND THEY ARE ADVISING HER TO RETURN WITH THEM.

"OH, VAL, ADVISE ME. MY PRESENCE IS NEEDED IN THE MISTY ISLES, BUT I SHALL NOT GO IF YOU FORBID IT." VAL SMILES: "THE FIRST DUTY OF ROYALTY IS TO THEIR PEOPLE. IS THAT WHAT YOU EXPECTED ME TO SAY?"
"YES," SHE GRINS, "YOU ARE SO PREDICTABLE. THAT IS WHY I LOVE YOU!"

VAL RETURNS TO THE KING. "WITH YOUR LEAVE, SIRE, I GO TO THE MISTY ISLES, AND ON MY WAY WILL PASS CLOSE BY DATHRAM WHERE BALDA HAN HOLDS SIR GAWAIN FOR RANSOM. I COULD STOP OFF AND MAKE TERMS FOR HIS RELEASE."

"THE KING HAS GIVEN ME LEAVE TO SAIL WITH YOU, AS I WILL HAVE A BIT OF BUSINESS TO ATTEND TO ALONG THE WAY."

1607   © King Features Syndicate, Inc., 1967. World rights reserved.   11-26

THE WINTER STORMS ARE BEGINNING TO BLOW AND THE SEA VOYAGE IS A ROUGH ONE. BUT THE WINDS COME OUT OF THE NORTH AND WEST AND IN A VERY FEW WEEKS THEY PASS THE MIST-SHROUDED PILLARS OF HERCULES AND ENTER THE INLAND SEA.

NEXT WEEK—Dathram

Our Story: ON THE OCEAN THERE IS NO ENEMY EXCEPT THE OCEAN ITSELF, BUT THE MEDITERRANEAN IS SCOURGED BY FIERCE CORSAIRS, AND ESCORT VESSELS FROM THE MISTY ISLES ARE WAITING THERE TO ESCORT QUEEN ALETA HOME.

NOW PRINCE VALIANT EXPLAINS HIS PLANS TO HIS FAMILY. IN ONE OF THE SMALLER VESSELS HE WILL SAIL FOR DATHRAM AND TRY TO ARRANGE FOR THE RANSOM OF SIR GAWAIN, IF HE STILL LIVES. WHEN HIS MISSION IS COMPLETED HE WILL JOIN THEM IN THE MISTY ISLES.

NO SOUND OF LAUGHTER OR MUSIC COMES FROM DATHRAM'S SEAPORT. IT IS A SLAVE MARKET, A CITY WITHOUT A SOUL DEALING IN HUMAN MISERY AND DESPAIR. THEIR SHIP GLIDES IN AND MOORS AT THE QUAY.

VAL'S GUIDE LEADS HIM TO THE GOVERNOR'S PALACE, AND THAT SHREWD OFFICIAL APPRAISES HIS VISITOR'S JEWELLED SWORD HILT, GOLDEN NECKLACE AND ARMBANDS BEFORE SPEAKING: "A CARAVAN WILL LEAVE ON THE MORROW TO TAKE THE WEALTH OF PLUNDERED CITIES TO OUR GLORIOUS MASTER, BALDA HAN, EMPEROR OF ALL DATHRAM. YOU MAY TRAVEL WITH IT."

HORSES ARE PROVIDED AND THE CARAVAN WINDS ITS WAY ACROSS THE BITTER DESERT UNDER A GLARING SUN. IN THE REAR AMID THE CHOKING DUST COME THE HOPELESS SLAVES IN SILENCE, SAVE FOR THE RATTLE OF CHAINS, THE CRACK OF WHIPS, AND CRIES OF PAIN.

AS HE LEADS THE CARAVAN ACROSS THE DESERT BY SECRET WAYS THE GOVERNOR PONDERS: "THIS WARRIOR FROM KING ARTHUR'S COURT HAS JEWELS AND GOLD. HE MIGHT ALSO CARRY THE RANSOM MONEY, AND IT ALL COULD BE MINE."

NEXT WEEK— Another Slave

1608

12-3

Our Story: THE DESERT SUN IS TERRIBLE, AND PRINCE VALIANT, USED TO THE FRESH COOL WINDS OF THULE AND BRITAIN, SUFFERS GREATLY.

AT NOON TENTS ARE SET UP AND THEY REST IN THE SHADE AND FIND SHELTER FROM THE BLOWING SAND.

IN THE AFTERNOON THE CARAVAN MOVES ON AGAIN UNTIL DARK. THE GOVERNOR INVITES VAL TO SHARE HIS EVENING MEAL, NOT BECAUSE OF HOSPITALITY, BUT ONCE MORE TO APPRAISE HIS GUEST'S WEALTH.

SATISFIED THAT THE JEWELS IN THE HILT AND SCABBARD OF THE 'SINGING SWORD' ARE GENUINE AND THE ORNAMENTS ARE REAL GOLD, HE GIVES ORDERS TO SOME MEN WHO ARE SUBTLE IN THE WAYS OF MURDER AND THE TAKING OF MEN.

IN THE HOUR BEFORE DAWN THE DEED IS DONE IN SILENCE, AND VAL IS STRIPPED AND BOUND. ALL HIS VALUABLES ARE TAKEN TO THE GOVERNOR.

"WHERE IS THE RANSOM MONEY?" DEMANDS THE GOVERNOR. "DO YOU SUPPOSE I WOULD CARRY IT INTO THIS NEST OF THIEVES?" ANSWERS VAL. "THE RANSOM MONEY WILL COME IN AN ARMED SHIP AND BE DELIVERED WHEN SIR GAWAIN IS SAFE ABOARD."

1609

THE HOT WIND BLOWS AND BLOWS AND THE WHISPERING SAND FILLS DRY NOSTRILS, CRACKS PARCHED LIPS. WHIPS CRACK, SLAVES CRY OUT, BUT VAL HOLDS HIMSELF ERECT AND STAGGERS FORWARD ON BLISTERED FEET AND SUCH HATRED IN HIS HEART AS NO MAN SHOULD FEEL.

NEXT WEEK – The Water Hole   12-10

Our Story: AT LAST THE TERRIBLE DAY ENDS, AND IN THE COOL OF THE EVENING THE SLAVES FIND REST. AND PRINCE VALIANT PLANS: SIR GAWAIN MUST BE RESCUED, THE 'SINGING SWORD' RECOVERED, AND THE HUMILIATION OF THE LASH REVENGED.

NEXT DAY VAL LOWERS HIS PROUD HEAD AND SHUFFLES ALONG LIKE THE OTHER SLAVES. EXHAUSTION, THIRST AND SUNBURN MAKE THE ACTING EASY.

LATE THE NEXT DAY THE CARAVAN APPROACHES A DEPRESSION IN THE MONOTONOUS DESERT, AND AT THE LOWER END.....A LAKE! EVEN THE SLAVES SHOUT FOR JOY, WHILE THE SLAVE MASTERS PREPARE FOR A GOOD LAUGH.

THE SLAVES ARE ALLOWED TO RACE TO THE SLIME-COVERED WATER AND PLUNGE THEIR FACES INTO IT, ONLY TO STRAIGHTEN UP AGAIN IN DISGUST AND SPIT IT OUT. THE SLAVE MASTERS ROAR WITH GLEE....IT IS SALT WATER!

IN THE CLIFF ABOVE THE SALT LAKE IS A SPRING, AND HERE THE CARAVAN REPLENISHES ITS WATER SUPPLY. IT IS DARK WHEN THEY ARE FINISHED, AND THEN THE SLAVES ARE AT LAST ALLOWED TO DRINK THEIR FILL.

THIRST, HEAT AND WEARINESS TAKE THEIR TOLL. VAL HAS LOST TRACK OF THE DAYS. BUT THERE IS HOPE. A FAINT LINE OF HILLS TAKES FORM IN THE DISTANCE, THE HILLS OF DAG! OH! IF ONLY A BREEZE WOULD BLOW FROM THOSE FAR FAINT HILLS!

THE WAY SLOPES UPWARD, GREENERY APPEARS, THEN TREES AND GARDENS. A CITY COMES INTO VIEW, ITS TOWERS AND TURRETS GLEAMING ALL WHITE IN THE SUNLIGHT. BRONZE GATES OPEN AND THE CARAVAN ENTERS THE STRONG-HOLD OF THE GREAT BALDA HAN.

NEXT WEEK — Sir Gawain is Found

1610

12-17

Our Story: THE CARAVAN ENTERS THE CITY OF BALDA HAN AND THE SLAVES ARE PARADED BEFORE THE OVERSEER. ALL THOSE WHO HOLD THEIR HEADS HIGH OR, BY THEIR SCARS AND MUSCLES SHOW THEM TO BE WARRIORS, ARE SET ASIDE AS HAVING TOO MUCH SPIRIT TO MAKE GOOD SLAVES.

TO BREAK THEIR SPIRITS THEY ARE STRIPPED AND TIED TO POSTS IN THE BLAZING SUN. VAL'S WHITE SKIN TURNS CRIMSON, BLISTERS FORM, AND TO MAKE MATTERS WORSE, THE PLAYFUL GUARDS BET ON WHO CAN BREAK THE BIGGER ONES WITH A FLICK OF THE LASH.

AT DAY'S END THE FIELD WORKERS COME IN SINGING. AND THE SONG THEY MUST SING IS THE 'SLAVE SONG!' THIS PREVENTS THEM FROM WHISPERING TOGETHER. THE LAST ONE SINGS IN THE CELTIC LANGUAGE, "PRETEND, PRETEND AND THE TORTURE WILL END. BEG FOR MERCY AND WHINE, AND WE'LL YET BEAT THE SWINE."

HE LIMPS, ONE ARM SWINGS USELESS, BUT THOSE BROAD SHOULDERS AND MUSCULAR LEGS? SIR GAWAIN! THEREAFTER VAL PRETENDS. HE PLEADS FOR MERCY, SCREAMS IN PAIN AND WHIMPERS. THE OVERSEER, SATISFIED THAT HIS SPIRIT IS BROKEN, ORDERS HIS RELEASE.

IN THE NIGHT VAL AND GAWAIN AT LAST COME TOGETHER. "ARE YOU SERIOUSLY CRIPPLED?" ASKS VAL. "NO," ANSWERS GAWAIN, "I BUT PRETEND, TO AVOID THE DEADLY LABOR AT THE QUARRIES."
"I TOO AM ILL," GRINS VAL AS HE PRACTICES WITH A HACKING COUGH. "THE DESERT SAND HAS HURT MY LUNGS."

"THE SLAVES OUTNUMBER THE GUARDS TEN TO ONE BUT THEY ARE WITHOUT HOPE. IF WE COULD ONLY COME BY SOME WEAPONS, THE DESIRE FOR REVENGE MIGHT OVERCOME THEIR DESPAIR."

NEXT DAY VAL, COUGHING LUSTILY, IS ASSIGNED TO THE SAME WORK GANG AS GAWAIN.

NEXT WEEK—**The Bronze Sword**

1611   © King Features Syndicate, Inc., 1967. World rights reserved.   12-24

Our Story: PRINCE VALIANT, WHO HAS JOURNEYED TO THE LAND OF DATHRAM TO ARRANGE RANSOM FOR SIR GAWAIN, NOW FINDS HIMSELF A SLAVE. HE WHO HAS KNOWN KINGS AND TROD THE MARBLE FLOORS OF PALACES IS NOW WITHOUT A NAME, FORCED TO WORK UNTIL RELEASED BY DEATH.

BECAUSE THE FAVORITE WIFE OF BALDA HAN DESIRES A GARDEN WITH A WATERFALL, A THOUSAND SLAVES TOIL UNDER A MERCILESS SUN. VAL LOOKS AROUND, NO GUARD IS WATCHING. "DO NOT DIG THERE, GAWAIN, YOU ARE UNCOVERING HEWN STONE," HE WHISPERS. "LET US FIND OUT WHAT IS BEYOND, IN SECRET."

AT DAYS END A HORN BLOWS, THE GUARDS CRACK THEIR WHIPS, AND THE SLAVES RAISE THEIR VOICES IN THE DISMAL 'SLAVE SONG' AS THEY GO TO THEIR PENS. VAL HAS CONTRIVED TO DIG A SHALLOW TRENCH BENEATH A BANK, AND WITH A FEW STROKES OF A MATTOCK, GAWAIN COVERS HIM UP.

WHEN ALL IS STILL VAL REMOVES A STONE AND REACHES INTO THE HOLLOW BEHIND. A CRYPT! FIRST HE REMOVES AN ANCIENT SKULL. THE RICH HELMET WITH MANY SCARS ON IT PROCLAIMS THE OWNER A WARRIOR OF RENOWN. VAL EXPLORES FURTHER.....

.....AND BRINGS FORTH A MIGHTY SWORD. THE BRONZE BLADE IS GREEN WITH AGE BUT STILL STRONG, ITS EDGE KEEN.

"ANCIENT WARRIOR, I HAVE DISTURBED YOUR LONG SLEEP BUT YOUR MIGHTY BLADE HAS YET SOME WORK TO DO ERE I RETURN IT TO YOUR SIDE."

  12-31

"I HAVE FOUND A SWORD AND HIDDEN IT. NOW THERE IS HOPE. FOR IT IS A GREAT SWORD AND WITH IT WE MUST DESTROY BALDA HAN AND HIS EVIL CITY!"

NEXT WEEK—Hope

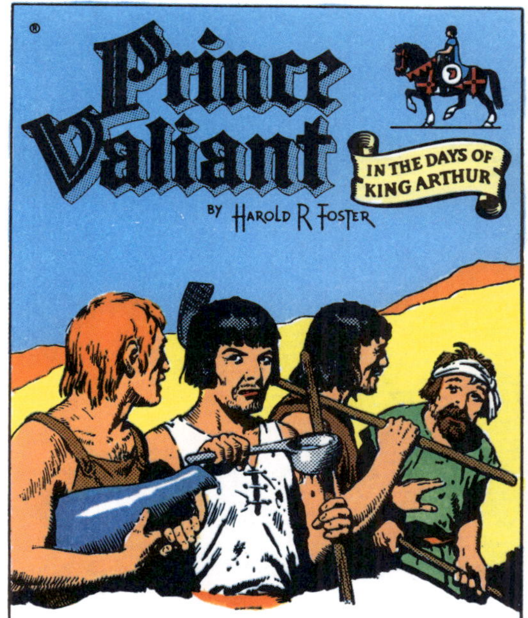

Our Story: ONE DAY OF MISERY FOLLOWS ANOTHER, BUT NOW VAL AND GAWAIN ASK A QUESTION: "WOULD YOU FIGHT FOR YOUR FREEDOM IF YOU HAD A WEAPON?"

THE MESSAGE SPREADS. "WE HAVE FOUND A LEADER WHO SAYS THE SLAVES OUTNUMBER THE GUARDS TEN TO ONE. WILL YOU FIGHT IF HE FINDS US WEAPONS?"

EVEN IN THE QUARRIES, WHERE THE TOIL IS SO TERRIBLE THAT THE VULTURES SIT AND WAIT, THERE COMES A GLEAM OF HOPE.

ONCE AGAIN A CARAVAN CROSSES THE DESERT COMING UP FROM THE SEA, BRINGING THE PLUNDER OF THE CORSAIRS AND GUIDED BY THE GOVERNOR. AND THE GOVERNOR IS QUITE HAPPY. HE WEARS 'THE SINGING SWORD' AND VAL'S GOLDEN NECKLACE. HE HOPES HIS LABORS WILL BRING A RICH REWARD.

HE SITS WITH HIS MASTER, BALDA HAN, WHO REMARKS: "IT HAS BEEN MANY MONTHS SINCE WE SENT A MESSENGER TO KING ARTHUR TO COLLECT RANSOM FOR SIR GAWAIN. HAVE YOU HEARD NOTHING OF IT?" "OH, NO, MASTER," ANSWERS THE SHIFTY-EYED GOVERNOR, "YOU KNOW THOSE COLD NORTHERN KINGS. THEY IGNORE YOUR POLITE REQUEST."

NOW THE TIME HAS COME. VAL HAS FELT THE LASH THAT DAY AND HIS FACE IS ALIGHT WITH THE LUST FOR BATTLE AS HE TAKES THE SWORD FROM ITS HIDING PLACE.

NEAR DAY'S END THE OFFICERS OF THE GUARDS SLIP AWAY TO ENJOY SHADE AND REFRESHMENT, AND THE GUARDS, FREED OF AUTHORITY, FIND A SHELTER FROM THE SUN AND PLAY AT DICE. UPON THE SWORD OF A LONG-DEAD WARRIOR HANGS THE FATE OF BALDA HAN AND HIS EVIL EMPIRE.

NEXT WEEK— To Arms!

1613   © King Features Syndicate, Inc., 1968. World rights reserved.   1-7

Prince Valiant
IN THE DAYS OF KING ARTHUR
BY HAROLD R FOSTER

Our Story: PRINCE VALIANT HEFTS THE ANCIENT SWORD, TESTING ITS BALANCE. IT IS A GOODLY BLADE AND IT SEEMS EAGER FOR ONE MORE BATTLE. CLOSER AND CLOSER HE AND SIR GAWAIN CREEP TO THE SLAVE GUARDS.

THE GUARDS ARE INTENT UPON THE DICE, NEVER EVEN DREAMING THAT THE SLAVES WOULD DARE REBEL. BULLIES ALL, THEY TURN CRAVEN BEFORE THE FEROCITY OF THE TWO WARRIORS AND OFFER LITTLE RESISTANCE.

SOME OF THE MORE STALWART SLAVES ARE ARMED WITH THE GUARDS' WEAPONS. NOW THEY HAVE A LEADER TO FOLLOW, AND HOPE RISES AS THEY TAKE UP THEIR MATTOCKS, SHOVELS AND SLEDGE HAMMERS.

JUST AS THEY HAVE, EVERY EVENING FOR YEARS PAST, THE SLAVES COME IN SINGING THE DISMAL 'SLAVE SONG' WHILE THE SENTRIES YAWN AND TAKE THEIR EASE.

AFTER THE SENTRIES ARE SLAIN, VAL AND GAWAIN HOLD COMMAND UNTIL THE ARMORY IS OPENED. NOW ARMED, THE SLAVES RAMPAGE THROUGH THE CITY SEEKING VENGEANCE FOR THE TERRIBLE DAYS OF SLAVERY UNDER THE LASH. THEY HAVE BECOME FIENDS OF BALDA HAN'S MAKING.
© King Features Syndicate, Inc., 1968. World rights reserved.
1614

HAL FOSTER
IN HIS LUXURIOUS PALACE BALDA HAN HEARS THE UPROAR AND COMMANDS HIS SECRETARY TO HAVE THE NOISE STOPPED, AS HE WISHES TO TAKE A NAP.
NEXT WEEK— The Return of 'The Singing Sword.'

Our Story: THE CITY OF BALDA HAN, WITH ITS WHITE TOWERS, ITS PALACES AND GARDENS, LAY SAFE IN THE COOL SHADOW OF THE HILLS OF DAG, PROTECTED BY A BURNING DESERT THAT ONLY A FEW KNEW THE WAY ACROSS.

BUT NOW THAT CITY IS IN FLAMES AS THE FRENZIED SLAVES SEEK VENGEANCE FOR THEIR WRONGS.
"WE WILL BE HELD PRISONERS BY THE DESERT UNLESS A GUIDE CAN BE FOUND," SAYS VAL.
"WE KNOW A CARAVAN CAME IN WITH THE GOVERNOR AS GUIDE. WE MUST FIND HIM."

HE AND GAWAIN GATHER TOGETHER A FEW OF THE ARMED SLAVES AND FORCE THEIR WAY THROUGH THE SCREAMING MOB. THE PALACE GUARD, ALREADY IN PANIC, OFFERS LITTLE RESISTANCE....

.... AND THE GOVERNOR IS ROUTED OUT FROM THE PILLOWS UNDER WHICH HE IS HIDING. HE READILY GIVES UP THE 'SINGING SWORD.' THEN, DRESSED IN RAGS SO THE SLAVES WILL NOT KILL HIM, HE IS PUT IN A SAFE PLACE.

THE FATE OF BALDA HAN IS SWIFT AND TERRIBLE. WITHOUT MERCY HE IS THROWN TO THE MOB.

FOR THREE DAYS THE FREED SLAVES SATISFY THEIR HATE ON THE DOOMED CITY, LOOTING AND BURNING. THEN AS THEIR FURY ABATES THEY REMEMBER THE DESERT AND ITS HORRORS. WOULD THEY DARE THE BURNING SANDS, OR STARVE IN THE RUINED CITY?

TRUE TO HIS PROMISE TO THE SPIRIT OF THE DEAD WARRIOR, PRINCE VALIANT RETURNS THE ANCIENT SWORD TO THE CRYPT, REPLACES THE STONE, AND HAS THE TOMB BURIED UNDER A MOUND OF EARTH.

NEXT WEEK—Born to Slavery

Our Story: THE FREED SLAVES, HAVING SATISFIED THEIR VENGEANCE ON THEIR MASTERS, TURN THEIR ATTENTION TO PLUNDERING THE BURNING CITY. MOST OF THEM HAVE NEVER POSSESSED ANYTHING OF THEIR OWN AND THEIR GREED IS COMPLETE. TWENTY CARAVANS COULD NOT CARRY THE LOOT ACROSS THE SUN-BAKED DESERT.

VAL TALKS TO THE PROUD CAMELMEN AND THEY AGREE TO TAKE THEIR ANIMALS BEYOND THE WALLS AND GUARD THEM FROM THE DESPERATE SLAVES.

SIR GAWAIN IS CAUGHT UP IN THE LOOTING FEVER: "THESE ARE BALDA HAN'S DANCING GIRLS. AS YOU SEE, VAL, THEY ARE TOO PRECIOUS TO LEAVE BEHIND."

ON THE PLAINS OUTSIDE THE CITY WALLS THE SLAVES SIT DUMBLY ON THEIR HEAPS OF PLUNDER. THEY CAN ACT ONLY ON ORDERS FROM A MASTER AND ARE COMPLETELY UNABLE TO THINK FOR THEMSELVES. VAL WONDERS IF HE WAS RIGHT IN SETTING THEM FREE. THOSE WHO SURVIVE THE DESERT CROSSING WILL AGAIN BECOME SLAVES, FOR THEY KNOW NOTHING ELSE.

SIR GAWAIN HAS COLLECTED MORE THAN DANCING GIRLS. HE HAS GATHERED TOGETHER ALL THOSE WHOSE SPIRIT HAS NOT BEEN CRUSHED, AND NOW HE HAS AN ARMED TROOP TO KEEP ORDER.

THERE IS NOTHING LEFT TO EAT IN THE CHARRED CITY. THE DESERT CROSSING MUST BEGIN. THE GOVERNOR IS DRAGGED FROM HIS HIDING PLACE TO LEAD THE CARAVAN. ONLY HE KNOWS THE LANDMARKS THAT LEAD TO THE OASES. THERE ARE NO PATHS, FOR THE HOT WINDS EVER BLOW AND FILL THE TRACKS WITH SAND.

NEXT WEEK—*The Desert Lies in Wait*

1-28

1616

Our Story: THE CARAVAN IS READY TO START ACROSS THE DESERT THAT SEEMS TO LIE WAITING. PRINCE VALIANT HAS FREED THE SLAVES, BUT TO WHAT END? MANY HAVE DIED IN THE BATTLE FOR FREEDOM. HOW MANY MORE WILL THE FEVERED BREATH OF THE DESERT CLAIM?

"WE WILL START AT DAWN. THERE WILL BE NO ROOM ON THE CAMELS FOR YOUR PLUNDER. JEWELS AND GOLD YOU MAY TAKE AND A JUG OF WATER. ALL ELSE MUST BE ABANDONED." THE SLAVES LOOK AT HIM DULLY AS EACH CLINGS DESPERATELY TO THE ONLY POSSESSIONS HE HAS EVER OWNED.

AT NOON THE CAMELMEN SET UP TENTS TO ESCAPE THE MENACE OF THE MIDDAY SUN. NOW THE WISDOM OF SIR GAWAIN'S CHOICE OF PLUNDER, SIX DANCING GIRLS, IS QUITE APPARENT, AND HE IS THE ENVY OF ALL.

WHEN THE TIME COMES TO MOVE AGAIN THE STRAGGLERS ARE STILL STAGGERING IN, THEIR WATER SUPPLY CONSUMED LONG SINCE. WHEN ONE DISCARDS PART OF HIS BURDEN SOMEONE BEHIND SNATCHES IT UP AND ADDS IT TO HIS OWN. VAL CANNOT BEAR TO WATCH THEM.

IT TAKES TWO DAYS TO REACH THE FIRST OASIS. FROM A TOR VAL LOOKS BACK AT THE THIN LINE OF STRAGGLERS. "THE DESERT HAS TAKEN ITS TOLL. WE MUST SAVE AS MANY AS WE CAN, FOR THERE IS YET THE SEAPORT OF DATHRAM TO CONQUER."

1617   © King Features Syndicate, Inc., 1968. World rights reserved.   2-4

ALL NIGHT AND ALL THE NEXT DAY WATER IS CARRIED BACK ALONG THE ROUTE UNTIL A CLOUD OF VULTURES GIVES EVIDENCE THAT THERE WILL BE NOTHING BUT BLEACHED BONES ALL THE WAY BACK TO THE RUINED CITY.

NEXT WEEK— The Governor Rebels

Our Story: ALL NIGHT AND ALL THE NEXT DAY WATER IS CARRIED FROM THE OASIS TO THE STRAGGLING ARMY OF FREED SLAVES. ONCE REFRESHED THEY STAGGER ON, CLINGING WITH PATHETIC DESPERATION TO THEIR PLUNDER, ONLY TO FALL AGAIN UNDER ITS WEIGHT. "SLAVES," CONSIDERS VAL, "SLAVES, UNABLE TO THINK FOR THEMSELVES, USED ONLY TO OBEY ORDERS."

"DROP YOUR LOADS. CARRY ONLY YOUR WEAPONS AND WATER JUGS!" HE ORDERS, "LIFT YOUR HEADS AND MARCH. YOU ARE NO LONGER SLAVES BUT FREE MEN!"

IF ORDERS ARE ALL THEY UNDERSTAND, ORDERS THEY WILL GET. A FEW DAYS OF MERCILESS DRILLING AND VAL IS ACCEPTED AS THEIR MASTER. DURING THE BITTER YEARS OF SLAVERY THEY HAVE LEARNED TO FEAR ARMED MEN. NOW THEY CARRY WEAPONS, AND A FEELING ALMOST OF PRIDE REPLACES THE FEAR.

THE CARAVAN MOVES ON, BUT NOW THERE ARE NO STRAGGLERS, FOR VAL BRINGS UP THE REAR. AND THE DESERT, AS IF ANGRY AT BEING CHEATED OF ITS VICTIMS, SENDS HEAT, THIRST AND SANDSTORMS TO HARRY THEM.

ONE NIGHT WHEN STARS GLITTER AND THE CAMP IS SILENT, VAL DISCERNS A FAINT GLOW OF LIGHT WAY OFF TO THE NORTHEAST AND THE SOUND OF BELLS IS HEARD FROM AFAR. "THE SEAPORT OF DATHRAM!" EXCLAIMS GAWAIN. "TOMORROW WE TAKE IT OR DIE IN THE DESERT."

THE GOVERNOR IS AWAKENED AND TOLD WHAT HIS PART WILL BE IN GETTING THEM PAST THE CITY GATES.

2-11 © King Features Syndicate, Inc., 1968. World rights reserved. 1618

BUT, WHITE-FACED AND CRINGING, HE REFUSES. "I SAW THE AWFUL PILLAGE OF BALDA HAN'S CITY. I CANNOT BETRAY DATHRAM. MY WIFE AND SONS ARE THERE!"

NEXT WEEK — The Long Chance

Our Story: THE GOVERNOR REFUSES TO DO PRINCE VALIANT'S BIDDING. "DO NOT TRIFLE WITH ME," VAL SAYS GRIMLY. "YOU TOOK MY SWORD, MY NAME AND SOLD ME INTO SLAVERY!"
"I HAVE INDEED EARNED YOUR ANGER," WHIMPERS THE GOVERNOR, "BUT I WILL NOT BETRAY MY CITY."

BUT HE HAS SEEN THESE TWO NORTHERN KNIGHTS BRING DOWN BALDA HAN AND DESTROY HIS WALLED CITY, AND FEARS THEY WILL DO THE SAME TO DATHRAM WITHOUT HIS HELP. SO HE UNFOLDS A PLAN THAT MIGHT AVOID THE HORRORS OF PILLAGING.

AT TWILIGHT THE CARAVAN APPROACHES THE WALLS, AND THE GOVERNOR SIGNALS THE GATEKEEPERS TO OPEN THE GREAT IRON-STUDDED GATES.

THE LONG CARAVAN WINDS ITS WAY TO THE WIDE MARKET SQUARE AS USUAL, AND IF ANYONE NOTICES THAT THERE ARE A GREAT NUMBER OF ARMED STRANGERS, THEY ARE NOT ALARMED.

NOW THE GOVERNOR CALLS IN THE PATROLS ONE AT A TIME. A RUMOR HAS SPREAD THAT THEY WILL RECEIVE THEIR BACK PAY, SO THEY COME WILLINGLY. ONE BY ONE THEY ARE ADMITTED TO THE ARMORY AND DISARMED. BY NIGHTFALL THE ENTIRE GARRISON IS IMPRISONED.

THE WEAPONS ARE PILED IN THE MARKET PLACE AND ARE DISTRIBUTED TO SLAVES, BEGGARS AND POOR WORKERS. VAL IS CONFIDENT HE CAN CONTROL HIS ARMY OF FREED SLAVES. THEY ARE NOW THE ONLY ORGANIZED FORCE WITHIN THE WALLS AS THEY WAIT QUIETLY FOR HIS ORDERS.

BUT WHAT OF THE DENIZENS OF THE DARK ALLEYS? WITH WEAPONS IN THEIR HANDS THEY DO WHAT VAL EXPECTED. THEY FORM INTO GANGS AND, IN THE ABSENCE OF THE PATROLS, BEGIN TO ROB AND BURN. THE ALARM BELLS RING OUT.

NEXT WEEK — Tribute

© King Features Syndicate, Inc., 1968. World rights reserved.

Our Story: WHEN THE DIN OF RIOTING AND THE MOUNTING FLAMES HAVE AROUSED THE ENTIRE CITY, PRINCE VALIANT ORDERS HIS ARMED FOLLOWERS INTO POSITION, AND SIR GAWAIN TAKES COMMAND.

AND WITH DRAWN WEAPONS THEY KEEP THE VIOLENCE CONTAINED IN THE SLUMS OF THE WATERFRONT.

IN THE PALACES OF THE RICH MERCHANTS AND GOVERNMENT OFFICIALS THERE IS PANIC. NO ARMED GUARDS PATROL THE STREETS. THEIR SLAVES AND SERVANTS HAVE JOINED IN THE VIOLENCE.

THE CITY COUNCIL IS CALLED TO THE GOVERNOR'S PALACE. THEY COME IN HASTE ONLY TO HEAR SOME FEARFUL NEWS.
"TWO NORTHERN WARRIORS HAVE FORMED AN ARMY OF ARMED SLAVES AND DESTROYED THE MIGHTY BALDA HAN AND SACKED HIS HIGH-WALLED CITY."

VAL GIVES HIS ULTIMATUM: "YOUR ENTIRE GARRISON HAS BEEN DISARMED AND IMPRISONED IN THE ARMORY. I COMMAND THE ONLY ARMED TROOP WITHIN THE CITY. YOU WILL PAY TRIBUTE TO THE MEN YOU SOLD INTO SLAVERY OR I WILL ALLOW THEM TO SACK YOUR PALACES!"

ONE BY ONE THE NOBLES AND WEALTHY MERCHANTS ARE CALLED IN AND TRIBUTE LEVIED. ALTHOUGH THEY ONE AND ALL PLEAD POVERTY, THE GOVERNOR, HIDDEN BEHIND A SCREEN, WHISPERS WHAT EACH ONE IS WORTH, AND SEEMS TO TAKE A SLY PLEASURE IN THE PROCEEDINGS.

2-25

1620

"SIR VALIANT, I HAVE DONE YOUR BIDDING. THE CITY IS IN YOUR HANDS. YOU HAVE KEPT YOUR PROMISE NOT TO DESTROY IT. NOW KEEP YOUR OTHER PROMISE AND LET ME AND MY FAMILY GO FREE."

NEXT WEEK—'Paradise Lost'

Our Story: TRUE TO HIS PROMISE PRINCE VALIANT ALLOWS THE GOVERNOR TO DEPART WITH HIS FAMILY AND WHAT VALUABLES HE CAN GATHER TOGETHER. HE IS IN A HURRY, FOR MANY OF HIS FORMER ASSOCIATES ARE ALREADY SHARPENING THEIR DAGGERS.

AS CONQUEROR VAL REMAKES THE LAWS: FAIR WAGES TO THE WORKERS, JUST TAXES, A REPRESENTATIVE COUNCIL, A POLICE FORCE TO PROTECT THE POOR AS WELL AS THE RICH. HE FINALLY CREATES A GOVERNMENT THAT WILL BRING PROSPERITY TO ALL.

IT IS WITH PRIDE THAT VAL VIEWS THE WELL-ORDERED CITY. PERHAPS IT MAY ONE DAY BE A TRADING PORT INSTEAD OF A SLAVE MARKET. HE CAN BE FORGIVEN THE SMUG LOOK ON HIS FACE. HE WHO WAS RECENTLY A SLAVE HAS CONQUERED TWO WALLED CITIES.

VAL AND SIR GAWAIN SET SAIL FOR THE MISTY ISLES, AND AS SOON AS THEIR SHIP IS OUT OF SIGHT THE WILY MERCHANTS SET ABOUT CHEATING THE POPULACE, AND THE POLITICIANS PLAN TO INCREASE THE TAXES. IN A FEW DAYS THE CITY SETTLES BACK INTO THE COMFORTABLE CHEATING WAYS THAT IT WAS USED TO.

AND VAL'S ARMY OF FREED SLAVES? THEY WERE GIVEN A JUST SHARE OF THE TRIBUTE MONEY, AND NEVER HAVING HAD TO LEARN THE VALUE OF MONEY, IT SLIPS THROUGH THEIR FINGERS IN A FEW WEEKS OF RIOTOUS LIVING.

1621

3-3

NOW AT LAST THEY ARE ON THEIR WAY TO THE MISTY ISLES, AND ALTHOUGH GAWAIN'S SHARE OF THE PLUNDER (SIX DANCING GIRLS) IS A BIT OF A NUISANCE, THEY DO MAKE THE JOURNEY ENTERTAINING.

NEXT WEEK— Trouble in the Misty Isles

Our Story: ALETA, QUEEN OF THE MISTY ISLES, RETURNS TO HER KINGDOM TO FIND IT IN DEEP TROUBLE, BUT A TROUBLE HER PEOPLE ARE ENJOYING. OH, IF ONLY SHE HAD VAL AT HER SIDE TO LEND HER HIS STRENGTH!

EACH DAY SHE WALKS TO THE FAR WESTERN TIP OF THE ISLAND WHERE STANDS THE TEMPLE OF APHRODITE, AND THERE WATCHES THE SEA FOR SOME SIGN OF VAL'S LONG-OVERDUE SHIP.

AT LAST IT COMES FOAMING OVER THE BLUE SEA AND HER HEART LEAPS WITH GLADNESS.

AS VAL STEPS ASHORE THERE IS A FLASH OF GOLD, A SQUEAL OF DELIGHT, AND A PERFUMED BUNDLE LANDS IN HIS ARMS. THIS IS DECIDEDLY NOT THE WAY FOR A QUEEN TO GREET HER HUSBAND, BUT AT LEAST IT MAKES HIM FEEL WELCOME.

"MY KINGDOM IS DOOMED BY PROSPERITY. WEALTH HAS BECOME A BURDEN TO MY PEOPLE, AND THEY LOLL IN LUXURY. INDOLENCE IS A HABIT, AMUSEMENT THEIR ONLY BUSINESS. COME, I'LL SHOW YOU SOME EXAMPLES."

"WHO IS THAT?" ASKS VAL, "SOME PRINCELY GENERAL?" "NO," ANSWERS ALETA, "THAT IS BUT A COMMON SOLDIER. OUR OFFICERS DRESS LIKE PEACOCKS, BUT THEY DANCE DIVINELY!"

"ONCE WE WERE THE FINEST SWIMMERS IN THE WORLD. NOW WE LIE BESIDE HEATED POOLS WITH PERFUMED WATER, AND EAT AND DRINK THE WHOLE DAY THROUGH."

1622

3-10

"NOW, THERE IS ONE OF OUR GREATEST ATHLETES. HE WILL DINE WITH US TONIGHT, AND WHEN HE SPEAKS OF HIS PROWESS I BEG YOU NOT TO LAUGH."
NEXT WEEK— **The Athletes**

Our Story: PRINCE VALIANT, REMEMBERING HOW SIMPLE AND FREE LIFE HAD BEEN THREE YEARS AGO WHEN LAST HE VISITED THE MISTY ISLES, IS SURPRISED AND A BIT DISAPPOINTED AT ALL THE NEW LUXURY AND INDOLENCE HE MEETS. SEATED BESIDE HIM AT THE BANQUET IS KNOSSES, RENOWNED AS AN ATHLETE.....

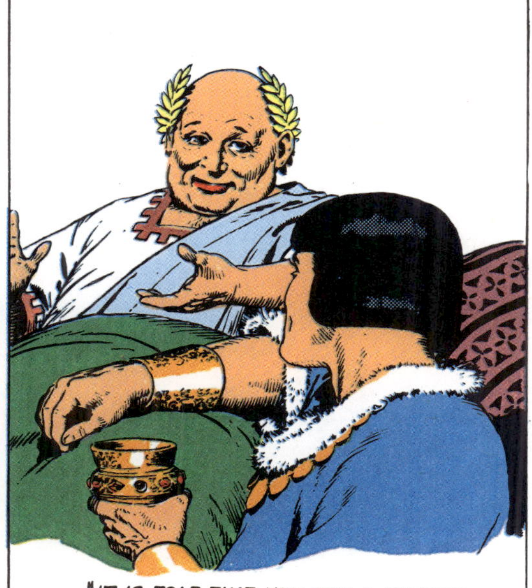

"GREATEST, FIDDLESTICKS!" INTERRUPTS MILTHOS FROM THE OTHER SIDE. "I WILL WAGER YOU WILL BREATHE MY DUST ALL AROUND THE STADIUM TRACK..... PROVIDED YOU CAN GO THAT FAR!"

KNOSSES LEAPS TO HIS FEET IN ANGER: "YOUR MOUTH STIRS MORE DUST THAN YOUR HEELS.... TRIPLE THE DISTANCE AND TRIPLE THE WAGER AND I WILL MEET YOU IN THE STADIUM TOMORROW!"

"I CANNOT BELIEVE MY EYES," SAYS A PUZZLED VAL. "NEITHER KNOSSES OR MILTHOS APPEARS FIT FOR ANYTHING MORE STRENUOUS THAN LIFTING A GOBLET. THEY WHEEZE WHEN THEY RISE FROM THE COUCH."

1623
© King Features Syndicate, Inc., 1968. World rights reserved.
3-17

AS THE NOBLES DO NOT ARISE UNTIL NOON, THE CONTEST IS HELD IN THE COOL OF THE AFTERNOON. VAL AND ALETA JOIN THE THRONG GOING TO THE ARENA.

NEXT WEEK—The Foot Race

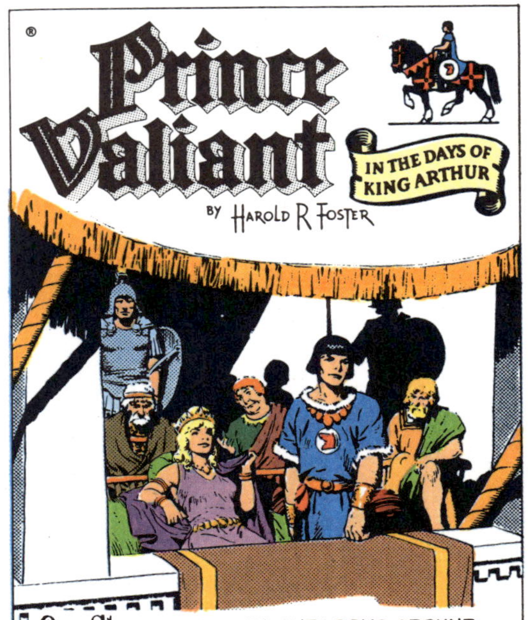

Our Story: PRINCE VALIANT LOOKS AROUND THE VAST NEW STADIUM AND HE WONDERS. THOSE TWO RENOWNED ATHLETES, KNOSSES AND MILTHOS, ARE SO FAT AND DISSIPATED HE DOUBTS IF THEY CAN WALK ACROSS THE TRACK, LET ALONE RACE FOR THREE LAPS.

THEN KNOSSES COMES OUT ON THE TRACK CARRIED BY EIGHT SINEWY NUBIANS AND RAISES HIS WHIP IN SALUTE TO ALETA, QUEEN OF THE MISTY ISLES.

MILTHOS FOLLOWS WITH A TEAM OF GREAT-THEWED GOTHS. SO THE MYSTERY IS SOLVED. UNCONTROLLED PROSPERITY HAS BROUGHT SUCH LUXURY LIVING THAT THE NOBLE ATHLETES HIRE OTHERS TO DO THEIR RACING, WRESTLING AND JUMPING FOR THEM.

THE RACE BEGINS AND ON THE FIRST LAP THE LITHE NUBIANS DRAW AHEAD. DURING THE SECOND THEY HOLD THE LEAD BUT BEGIN TO FALTER UNDER THE WEIGHT OF THE MASTER ATHLETE. AS THE THIRD LAP STARTS, THE THUNDERING GOTHS SLOWLY GAIN UNTIL THEY ARE NECK AND NECK....THEN!

.... KNOSSES RISES IN HIS SEAT AND LAYS ABOUT WITH HIS WHIP, UPSETTING THE RHYTHM OF THE RUNNERS. THE LITTER SWAYS, CREAKS, AND WITH A SPLINTERING CRASH COLLAPSES.

CAUGHT IN THE WRECKAGE, KNOSSES BOUNDS ALONG, THE FIRST EXERCISE HE HAS HAD IN YEARS, AND RELIEVED OF HIS GREAT WEIGHT, THE NUBIANS RACE AHEAD AND CROSS THE FINISH LINE THE WINNERS.

WHEN HE FINALLY RECOVERS ENOUGH TO SPEAK, HE GASPS: "MY RACING DAYS ARE OVER. I'LL NEVER RUN AGAIN!"

1624   © King Features Syndicate, Inc. 1968. World rights reserved.   3-24

"A RIDICULOUS SIGHT, BUT I COULD CRY," SIGHS ALETA. "WEALTH HAS BROUGHT ONLY LUXURY, GLUTTONY AND SLOTH. OUR WEALTH IS THE ENVY OF OUR NEIGHBORS, BUT WE ARE TOO WEAK TO DEFEND IT."

NEXT WEEK— Rumors

Our Story: HOW CAN A SMALL QUEEN SAVE HER KINGDOM WHEN ITS ONLY PROBLEM IS PROSPERITY? IT IS THE ILLS THAT WEALTH CAN BRING THAT CAUSE HER DISMAY: INDOLENCE, DISSIPATION AND SLOTH.

IN THE GARB OF A PEDDLER PRINCE VALIANT WANDERS THROUGH THE BAZAAR AND LEARNS MANY THINGS. THERE IS LITTLE WEALTH HERE. LABOR IS DONE BY UNPAID SLAVES, STORE-KEEPERS ARE TAXED BEYOND REASON, ARTISANS WORK LONG HOURS.

A TALKATIVE SHOPKEEPER TELLS HIM: "THESE ARE THE RICHEST ISLANDS IN THE AEGEAN SEA, BUT THE WEALTHY MERCHANTS AND NOBLES HAVE IT ALL!" THEN, WITH A SLY WINK, "BUT NOT FOR LONG, FRIEND, THERE ARE RUMORS.....!"

QUEEN ALETA IS THOUGHTFUL, AT LAST SHE SPEAKS: "YOU CONQUERED BALDA HAN'S WALLED CITY WITH AN ARMY OF SLAVES YOU HAD FREED. PERHAPS THE SAME STRATEGY WILL WORK FOR ME. BRING ME THAT TALKATIVE SHOPKEEPER."

AND THE SHOPKEEPER, OVERAWED BY THE PRESENCE OF THE QUEEN, TALKS LONG AND FEARFULLY ABOUT THE RUMORS HE HAS HEARD. CRAFTSMEN ARE LEAVING FOR OTHER LANDS, SAILORS DESERT THE NAVY FOR MORE PROFITABLE EMPLOYMENT, CORSAIRS HARRY THE SHIPPING AND RICH MERCHANTS PURCHASE TITLES.

"GO BACK TO THE LOWER TOWN AND FIND ME SIX WISE MEN WHO ARE LEADERS IN THIS DISCONTENT, MEN WHO BELIEVE THEIR QUEEN IS JUST."

"NOW YOU TWO BOYS GO OUT AND PLAY, BUT DON'T FORGET TO LEARN WHAT OUR GENTRY THINK, IF AT ALL. AND GAWAIN, STAY AWAY FROM THE LADIES FOR JUST A LITTLE LONGER!"

"AN ELFIN BLONDE ORDERS THE GREATEST KNIGHT IN CHRISTENDOM AND HIS EX-SQUIRE PRINCE VALIANT TO DO HER BIDDING, AND WITHOUT QUESTION THEY DO. I SUSPECT THAT UNDER THOSE GOLDEN CURLS AN IDEA IS HATCHING, ONE SO SIMPLE NO MAN WOULD THINK OF IT."

NEXT WEEK – **The Reins of Command**

Our Story: WHEN, AFTER A LONG ABSENCE, QUEEN ALETA RETURNED TO HER SMALL KINGDOM, SHE TOOK HER THRONE BUT DID NOTHING TO STAY THE GREED, THE LUXURY AND INDOLENCE THAT WERE SLOWLY DRAINING HER ISLANDS OF STRENGTH.

QUIETLY SHE TAKES UP THE REINS OF GOVERNMENT. AMBASSADORS ARE RECALLED TO BRING INFORMATION AS TO WHICH OF THEIR ENVIOUS NEIGHBORS MIGHT BE TEMPTED TO INVADE.

TRUE TO HIS PROMISE THE LITTLE SHOPKEEPER BRINGS MEN FROM THE LOWER TOWN TO TELL OF THEIR DISCONTENT.

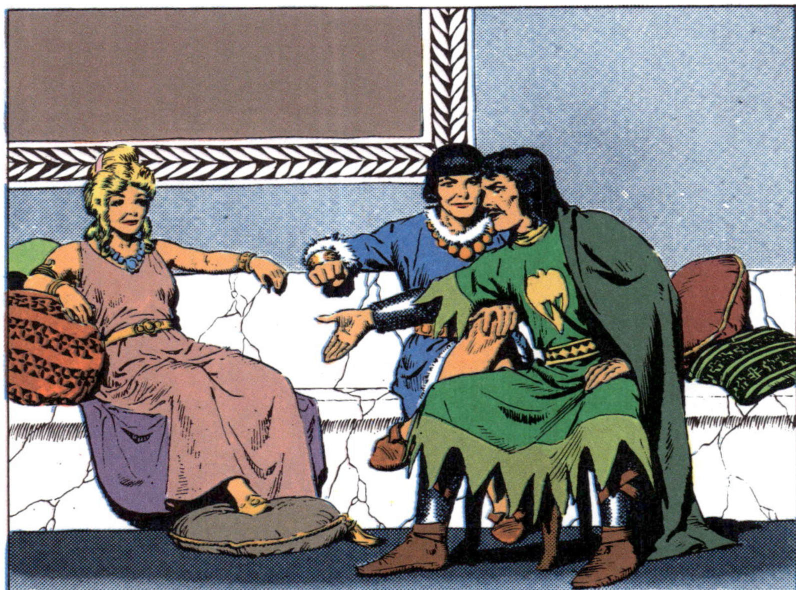

VAL AND GAWAIN RETURN FROM THE OFFICERS' GYMNASIUM. "POPINJAYS!" EXCLAIMS GAWAIN, "NOT ONE OF THEM PRACTICES THE WARRIOR'S SKILLS. THEY TRAIN JUST ENOUGH TO HAVE BEAUTIFUL BODIES SO THEY CAN WEAR THEIR GORGEOUS UNIFORMS GRACEFULLY. BAH!"

ALETA SEEKS ADVICE FROM HER OLD CHANCELLOR. "I HAVE BEEN RETIRED AND A NEW CHANCELLOR PUT IN MY PLACE, AND HE HAS MADE LAWS THAT BENEFIT THE RICH. BUT ONE LAW, MADE LONG AGO, HAS BEEN OVERLOOKED. IT STATES THAT NO HIGH OFFICE CAN BE AWARDED WITHOUT CONSENT OF THE CROWN."

THE QUEEN SITS SILENT FOR A WHILE, THEN A SLOW SMILE BRIGHTENS HER FACE. "YOU MAY ONCE AGAIN BE MY COUNCILOR."

A COURIER ARRIVES. "YOUR MAJESTY, CORSAIRS ARE ATTACKING OUR MERCHANT VESSELS. OUR NAVY IS PREPARING TO DRIVE THEM OFF."

VAL DONS HIS ARMOR AND HURRIES TO THE HARBOR. A GOOD FIGHT WOULD BE A RELIEF FROM ALL THIS INTRIGUE AND STATECRAFT.

NEXT WEEK – Bathtub Navy

Our Story: THE NEWS THAT PIRATES ARE ATTACKING THE MERCHANT FLEET BRINGS PRINCE VALIANT RACING TO BOARD ONE OF THE NAVY SHIPS TO SHARE IN THE FIGHTING. BUT HE NEED NOT HAVE HURRIED.....

...FOR, ALTHOUGH THE CREW WAS READY AND WAITING, THE OFFICERS COME ABOARD IN LEISURELY FASHION, AS IF IT IS BENEATH THEIR DIGNITY TO HURRY.

THE FINE WARSHIP HAS BEEN TURNED INTO A PLEASURE BARGE. THE HIGH TOP-HEAVY STERN CASTLE IS FITTED WITH GILDED CHAIRS AND BRIGHT AWNINGS, WHILE THE SAILORS ARE CROWDED INTO THE FORECASTLE LIKE CATTLE.

AS VAL WATCHES THE SAILING MASTER DESPERATELY TRYING TO BRING SOME ORDER OUT OF THE CROWDED DECK BELOW, HE SHOWS HIS DISGUST: "BOLTAR AND HIS CREW COULD TAKE THIS SHIP WITHIN AN HOUR, AND OUR WHOLE NAVY BEFORE SUNDOWN!"

A SMUDGE OF SMOKE ON THE HORIZON IS A SIGN THAT THE PIRATES ARE STILL BUSY WITH THE MERCHANT SHIPS. THE YOUNG OFFICERS SHOW THEIR INTEREST BY HAVING THEIR SERVANTS STRING THEIR BOWS FOR THEM AND PLACE PIKES, THROWING-SPEARS AND SHEAVES OF ARROWS AT HAND.

ONE SHIP DRIFTS BURNING. THE PIRATES ARE BUSY TRANSFERRING THE RICH CARGO OF ANOTHER TO THEIR OWN VESSEL. NOT UNTIL THE WARSHIP IS WITHIN BOWSHOT DO THEY LEAP INTO THEIR OWN SLEEK VESSEL AND, SHOUTING JEERS AND INSULTS, SAIL SWIFTLY AWAY.

4-14

1627

THE CAPTAIN STRIKES A HEROIC POSE: "LOOK AT THEM FLEE IN CONFUSION! ONCE AGAIN WE HAVE SINGLEHANDEDLY DRIVEN OFF THE RASCALS."

NEXT WEEK—The Raiders

Our Story: THE PLUNDERED MERCHANT SHIP DRIFTS AIMLESSLY WHILE THE CORSAIR WAITS IN THE DISTANCE TO FINISH LOOTING IT. TO VAL'S SURPRISE THE CAPTAIN GIVES ORDERS TO TAKE THE WARSHIP BACK TO THE HARBOR.

"ARE YOU GOING TO LEAVE THAT VESSEL FOR THE WAITING PIRATES?" ASKS VAL. "LOWER A BOAT, GIVE ME TWELVE MEN, AND I WILL BRING IT INTO PORT."
"BUT I NEED THE SAILORS TO HANDLE MY SHIP," THE CAPTAIN SAYS. "YOU HAVE TWENTY YOUNG OFFICERS WHO ARE DOING NOTHING," VAL INTERRUPTS. "ARE THEY NAVY MEN OR PASSENGERS?"

A BOAT IS LOWERED AND SIX OF THE OFFICERS VOLUNTEER, THINKING THIS MIGHT BE FUN. THEY GATHER IN THE STERN AND WAIT TO BE ROWED TO THE MERCHANT VESSEL....BUT NOT FOR LONG.

"TAKE TO THE OARS," VAL ORDERS AND, AS THEY HESITATE, ADDS, "AS THE WARSHIP DRAWS AWAY, THE CORSAIR COMES CLOSER AND TIME IS SHORT." TO RETURN WOULD MEAN FACING THE LAUGHTER OF THEIR FELLOW OFFICERS.... BETTER TO FACE THE DANGER AND BLISTERED HANDS.

THE DECK OF THE MERCHANT SHIP IS A GHASTLY SIGHT. THE PIRATES HAD QUIETED THE CREW WITH CRUEL ZEST. THE BODIES ARE COVERED WITH A CANVAS.

AS THE SAILORS STRUGGLE TO REPAIR THE TORN FORE SQUARE SAIL THE CORSAIR DRAWS EVER CLOSER. THEN, ONE BY ONE, THE OFFICERS REMOVE THEIR RESPLENDENT ARMOR AND JOIN THE CREW AT ITS BACK-BREAKING LABOR.

THE TOPHEAVY WARSHIP WALLOWS ON TOWARD PORT AND VAL WONDERS IF HE CAN GAIN ITS PROTECTION BEFORE THE PIRATE SHIP CLOSES IN TO FINISH ITS INTERRUPTED PLUNDERING. VAL DOES NOT KNOW THE TURMOIL THAT SEETHES IN THE BREAST OF THE WARSHIP'S CAPTAIN.

NEXT WEEK — The Captain's Dilemma

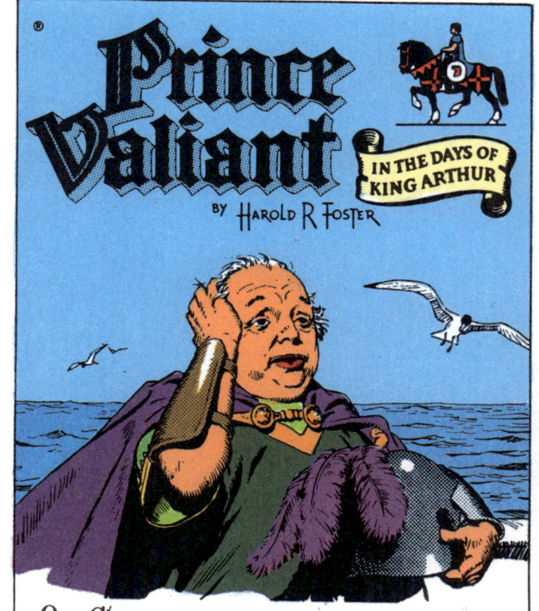

Our Story: NEVER, SINCE HE LEFT THE LOAN BUSINESS, HAS CAPTAIN SILUS HAD SUCH WORRIES. HE HAS A DINNER DATE WITH VERY IMPORTANT PEOPLE WHO MIGHT AID HIS ADVANCEMENT, AND PRINCE VALIANT, HUSBAND OF HIS QUEEN, IS DELAYING HIM.

THE CORSAIR IS GAINING ON VAL'S CRIPPLED SHIP AND, OH, DEAR! ON THAT SHIP ARE SIX YOUNG OFFICERS WHOSE WEALTHY PARENTS HAVE PAID WELL TO GET THEM THEIR POSITIONS!

THEN HE GETS AN IDEA.... A STROKE OF GENIUS! HE WILL MISS HIS APPOINTMENT, BUT RETURN A HERO!
"ARCHERS, STAND BY YOUR WEAPONS. SAILING MASTER, TURN THE SHIP AROUND. WE WILL RESCUE PRINCE VALIANT!"

AS THE PLUNDER WOULD NOT BE WORTH THE RISK, THE CORSAIR TURNS AWAY. CAPTAIN SILUS RAISES HIS MEGAPHONE: "YOU ARE SAFE NOW, PRINCE VALIANT, WE HAVE DRIVEN THEM OFF. FALL IN BEHIND ME AND WE WILL SAIL IN LINE INTO THE HARBOR."

VAL'S ANSWER COMES LOUD AND CLEAR. FOR FEAR OF CENSORSHIP WE WILL NOT PRINT IT HERE, BUT IT MAKES THE CAPTAIN'S EARS BURN AND BRINGS SMOTHERED LAUGHTER FROM THE CREW. AND VAL SAILS RIGHT BY AND INTO THE HARBOR.

THERE IS WEEPING AND WAILING AT THE QUAY AS FRIENDS AND RELATIVES CLAIM THE BODIES OF THE PIRATES' VICTIMS. A CRIME THAT CALLS FOR JUSTICE, BUT HOW? THE NAVY IS BUT A THEATRICAL FARCE, AND AS FOR MEN?-- VAL LOOKS AT THE YOUNG OFFICERS HE HAD CONSIDERED MILKSOPS. THEIR WHITE HANDS ARE STAINED AND BLISTERED FROM THE ROPES AND THEY ARE PUTTING THE SHIP IN ORDER.

1629

4-28

THEN HE REMEMBERS. THE SEA-GIRT MISTY ISLES WERE EVER FAMOUS FOR THEIR SAILORS, SWIMMERS AND PEARL DIVERS. GIVEN A CHANCE, THESE YOUTHS WOULD JOYOUSLY TAKE TO THE SEA.

NEXT WEEK — *The New Navy*

Our Story: WHEN IT IS TOLD AROUND THE WATERFRONT THAT PRINCE VALIANT IS PREPARING A SHIP TO RAID THE RAIDERS, MANY VOLUNTEERS FLOCK TO HIM — SEAFARERS AND FIGHTING MEN WHO LONG TO RESTORE THE FAME AND DIGNITY THAT THE MARINERS OF THE MISTY ISLES ONCE ENJOYED.

THE CORSAIRS HAVE BECOME SO BOLD THEY WAIT WITHIN A FEW MILES OFFSHORE. THEIR REWARD IS A MERCHANT SHIP, ITS DECKS CLUTTERED WITH BALES AND BOXES.

AS THE TWO SHIPS COME TOGETHER THE PIRATES SCREAM THEIR BATTLE CRY.....FOLLOWED QUICKLY BY ANOTHER CRY AS ARCHERS RISE FROM BEHIND THE BALES AND PIKEMEN POUR FROM THE HOLD. AND FROM THE CITY WALLS NEXT DAY HANG MANY PIRATES, AN OLD CUSTOM, EFFECTIVE, IF SLIGHTLY GRUESOME.

NOW VAL HAS TWO SHIPS TO FIGHT THE CORSAIRS, BUT THERE ARE DIFFICULTIES. CAPTAIN SILUS HAS COMPLAINED TO THE LORD HIGH ADMIRAL OF THE NAVY.
"SIR VALIANT, I MUST INFORM YOU THAT ALL CAPTURED SHIPS ARE THE PROPERTY OF THE NAVY," ANNOUNCES THE ADMIRAL.
"THE NAVY DID NOT CAPTURE THESE SHIPS, NOR IS IT CAPABLE OF CAPTURING ANY SHIPS," ANSWERS VAL PLEASANTLY.

"THE NAVY WILL NOT SUPPLY ANY MONEY TO OUTFIT THESE SHIPS AND I DEMAND YOU TURN THEM OVER TO ME!"
"I OUTFIT THEM AT MY OWN EXPENSE, BUT," HERE THE SMILE FADES FROM VAL'S FACE, "IF YOU WANT THEM, COME AND TAKE THEM!"

"IGNORANT YOUNG UPSTART. HE DOES NOT KNOW THERE IS MORE TO RUNNING A NAVY THAN JUST FIGHTING. HOWEVER, HE IS HUSBAND TO OUR QUEEN, SO WE WILL NOT ANGER HER BY TAKING HIS SHIPS AWAY."

IN HER PRIVATE CHAMBERS THE QUEEN SPENDS LONG HOURS WITH TRUSTED FRIENDS AND READERS OF THE LAW, TRYING TO UNTANGLE A SYSTEM THAT GIVES ALL POWER TO THE RICH.

NEXT WEEK—Another Victory

5-5   © King Features Syndicate, Inc., 1968. World rights reserved.   1630

Prince Valiant

IN THE DAYS OF KING ARTHUR

BY HAROLD R FOSTER

Our Story: QUEEN ALETA STUDIES THE LAWS SHE HERSELF HAS PASSED. LAWS INTENDED TO BRING PROSPERITY TO ALL THE PEOPLE OF THE MISTY ISLES. SOMEHOW THE SHREWD MERCHANTS HAVE PUT ON THESE LAWS A DIFFERENT INTERPRETATION THAT HAS MADE THEM RICH. SHE AND HER ADVISORS SPEND LONG HOURS UNTANGLING THE MESS.

MONTHS HAVE PASSED AND STILL THE QUEEN HAS NOT SOUGHT THE ADVICE OF THE COUNCIL.....AND THE MEMBERS OF THE COUNCIL ARE BECOMING NERVOUS. WHAT IS SHE UP TO? "A WOMAN IS NOT CAPABLE OF RULING," GRUMBLES KNOSSES, RICHEST OF THEM ALL. "WE SHOULD ELECT A REGENT, ONE LIKE OURSELVES WHO UNDERSTANDS BUSINESS! NOW I....." "SIT DOWN, KNOSSES," ANSWERS AENIOS, "I HAVE KNOWN THE QUEEN ALL HER LIFE. DO NOT LET A PRETTY FACE FOOL YOU."

ANOTHER THING WORRIES THEM. EVEN NOW, AND WITHOUT COSTING THE KINGDOM ONE COPPER COIN, PRINCE VALIANT IS SAILING OUT TO GIVE BATTLE TO THE CORSAIRS WHO RAID THE SHIPPING-- SOMETHING THEIR EXPENSIVE NAVY HAS NOT BEEN ABLE TO DO.

ONCE MORE A CORSAIR CHASES AND CATCHES A WALLOWING MERCHANT SHIP. THEIR INDULGENCE IN CRIME HAS AN UNHAPPY ENDING AS ARMED MEN POUR FROM THE HOLD AND PROVE TO THEM THAT A LIFE OF VIOLENCE IS A SHORT ONE.

AS VAL SAILS INTO THE HARBOR WITH STILL ANOTHER PRIZE THE WHOLE WATERFRONT RINGS WITH CHEERS. SMALL VICTORIES PERHAPS, BUT THEY AWAKEN THE OLD SEAFARING SPIRIT.

IS VAL BEING MEAN, OR IS IT JUST BY CHANCE THAT HE SAILS HIS PRIZE RIGHT UNDER THE STERNS OF THE ANCHORED NAVY? THE LORD HIGH ADMIRAL AND CAPTAIN SILUS LOOK ON. EACH HAS A SUDDEN ATTACK OF HEARTBURN.

THE PIRATE'S PLUNDER IS SOLD, THE PRIZE MONEY DIVIDED AMONG THE CREWS, AND NOW VAL MUST CHOOSE STILL ANOTHER CREW FROM AMONG THE HUNDREDS OF CLAMORING VOLUNTEERS.

NEXT WEEK— **The Council Meeting**

Our Story: QUEEN ALETA LEANS BACK WITH A SIGH. AT LAST SHE KNOWS THE VAUNTED PROSPERITY OF HER KINGDOM IS FALSE. ALL THE WEALTH IS IN THE HANDS OF A FEW, AND THOSE FEW HAVE TWISTED THE MEANING OF THE LAWS SHE HERSELF MADE TO THEIR OWN ADVANTAGE.

AFTER A WEEK OF SEARCHING AND FIGHTING VAL RETURNS TO PORT WITH HIS HEAVILY ARMED SHIPS. TWO MORE PIRATE VESSELS WILL BE ADDED TO THE FLEET WHILE TWO MORE DRIFT IN FLAMES. THE SEA IS JUST THAT MUCH SAFER FOR THE MARINERS OF THE MISTY ISLES.

AT LAST THE COUNCIL IS CALLED AND THE QUEEN, LOOKING VERY SMALL AND DAINTY, ASCENDS THE DAIS, BUT HER FIRST WORDS SEND A CHILL THROUGH THE MEMBERS.
"ON MY LAST VISIT WE WERE AT WAR. THE INVADERS WERE DRIVEN OFF AND WE CAPTURED THEIR TRANSPORT SHIPS. OUR GREAT PROSPERITY BEGAN WHEN THE VESSELS, THE PROPERTY OF THE STATE, WERE LOANED TO HONEST TRADERS WHO PAID A PERCENTAGE OF THEIR PROFITS. WHERE ARE THESE SHIPS NOW?"

"MY LORD HIGH ADMIRAL, YOU HAVE SIX OF THESE VESSELS. EXPLAIN."
"IT WAS ALL QUITE LEGAL," HE ANSWERS, MOPPING HIS BROW. "AS EVERYONE KNOWS, PRIVATE ENTERPRISE IS MORE PROFITABLE THAN GOVERNMENT OWNERSHIP. I PAID A FAIR PRICE AND HAVE SAVED THE KINGDOM THE COST OF UPKEEP."
"AND WHAT BECAME OF THE PURCHASE MONIES?"

"I USED IT TO BUILD THE MOST SPLENDID NAVY IN ALL THE AEGEAN SEA. THERE IS NONE MORE ELEGANT......" THE QUEEN INTERRUPTS: "THEN WE WILL REWARD YOU EVEN FURTHER. WE GIVE YOU SIX OF YOUR GRAND SHIPS-OF-WAR IN EXCHANGE FOR THE SIX MERCHANT VESSELS."

"BUT, MY LADY QUEEN, THE WARSHIPS ARE NOT FIT FOR TRADE....!" "THEY WERE, BEFORE YOU MADE THEM INTO GILDED PLAYTHINGS!" THE QUEEN INTERRUPTS.

5-19 © King Features Syndicate, Inc., 1968. World rights reserved. 1632

AGAIN ALETA CONSULTS HER NOTES.
"MY LORD KNOSSES WILL NOW EXPLAIN HOW HE, A WEALTHY MERCHANT, BECAME SUPREME COMMANDER OF OUR ARMY."

NEXT WEEK- Gifts! Gifts!

Our Story: THE LORD HIGH ADMIRAL SITS DOWN AND MOPS HIS BROW, HIS DREAMS SHATTERED. AGAIN QUEEN ALETA CONSULTS HER NOTES: "NOW WE ASK OUR GENERAL KNOSSES HOW HE, A WEALTHY MERCHANT, BECAME THE SUPREME COMMANDER OF OUR ARMY!"

KNOSSES, RICHEST MAN IN THE KINGDOM, IS NOT GOING TO BE TAKEN TO TASK BY A WOMAN, EVEN A QUEEN. "I WAS AWARDED THIS HIGH HONOR FOR MY PATRIOTISM, MY SERVICE TO THE KINGDOM AND GIFTS TO THE CITY," HE ANSWERS VIRTUOUSLY.

"'TWAS I WHO BUILT THE GREAT STADIUM AND GAVE IT AS A FREE GIFT TO THE CITY, A MONUMENT TO OUR GREATNESS!" HIS VOICE IS LOUD AND HE GLARES AT THE QUEEN. SHE IS GLANCING AT HER NOTES: "OUR RECORDS SHOW THAT THE STADIUM IS BUILT ON PUBLIC LAND AND THE CITY PAYS FOR ITS UPKEEP..... BUT YOU RETAIN ALL THE CONCESSIONS AND TICKET SALES. WE GIVE YOUR GIFT BACK TO YOU."

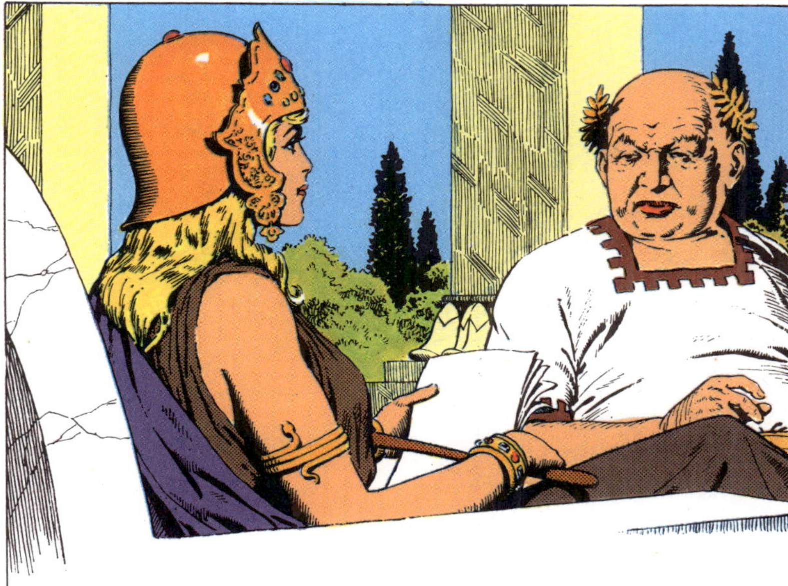

"WHAT CAN I DO WITH A STADIUM?" KNOSSES ROARS ANGRILY. "YOU CAN MOVE IT OFF GOVERNMENT LAND OR PAY A REASONABLE RENT..... AND TAXES." HER CALM GREY EYES MEET HIS ANGRY ONES, HE BLUSTERS BUT CANNOT MEET HER GAZE. HIS SHOULDERS SAG AND HE SITS DOWN. HE HAS MET A QUEEN.

AGAIN SHE REFERS TO HER NOTES, LOOKING UP NOW AND THEN TO FIX HER GAZE ON ONE OR ANOTHER OF THE NEWLY ELECTED COUNCIL MEMBERS, AND EACH ONE SQUIRMS IN HIS SEAT. "I WILL LEAVE YOU NOW THAT YOU MAY DISCUSS MY TWO EDICTS AND CAST YOUR BALLOTS."

TO THE LEFT OF THE COUNCIL CHAMBER SIT THE OLDER MEMBERS, NOBLES, WHO HAD NOT JOINED IN THE MAD SCRAMBLE FOR WEALTH, AND THEY LOOK WITH DELIGHT AT THE GROWING PANIC ON THE RIGHT.

THESE ARE THE NEWLY RICH WHO HOLD THE GREATER POWER, HONEST BUSINESSMEN ALL. BUT WOULD THE QUEEN MISTAKE A GIFT FOR A BRIBE? WOULD SHE THINK GOVERNMENT CONTRACTS A BIT HIGH PRICED? AND WHAT WAS IN THOSE CONFOUNDED NOTES OF HERS?

1633   © King Features Syndicate, Inc., 1968. World rights reserved.   5-26

ALETA RETURNS. HER EDICTS HAVE BEEN APPROVED, BUT BY THE NARROWEST MARGIN, AND SHE IS NOT PLEASED. "THE COUNCIL IS DISMISSED. I MUST GATHER FURTHER INFORMATION," AND SHE WAVES THOSE MYSTERIOUS NOTES. "WE MEET AGAIN IN THREE DAYS."

NEXT WEEK—Suspense

Our Story: ALETA, QUEEN OF THE MISTY ISLES, ENTERS THE COUNCIL CHAMBER LOOKING AS FRESH AND GENTLE AS THE SEA BREEZE THAT BLOWS IN THROUGH THE MARBLE COLUMNS. SHE DOES NOT TAKE THE THRONE BUT STANDS BEFORE THE COUNCIL, MUCH LIKE A SCHOOLTEACHER ADDRESSING A WAYWARD CLASS.

THE COUNCIL HAS HAD THREE UNCOMFORTABLE DAYS TO RE-EVALUATE THEIR DEEDS. WILL THEIR GENEROUS GIFTS BE CONSTRUED AS BRIBES, AND DOES THEIR QUEEN BELIEVE THE GREAT PROSPERITY THEY HAVE BROUGHT TO THE KINGDOM HAS GONE NO FURTHER THAN TO THEMSELVES? AND WHAT IS IN THAT SHEAF OF NOTES SHE HOLDS?

QUEEN ALETA PLUCKS THREE PAGES FROM HER NOTES. *"THE LORD HIGH ADMIRAL OF THE NAVY HAS RESIGNED."* (SHE BURNS ONE SHEET). *"SO HAS KNOSSES, SUPREME COMMANDER OF THE ARMY."* (ANOTHER NOTE IS FED TO THE FLAMES). THE THIRD SHE READS CAREFULLY BEFORE BURNING IT..

.....*"THE ONE YOU ELECTED LORD OF THE EXCHEQUER HAS BEEN REMISS IN HIS ACCOUNTS, SO WE HAVE GIVEN HIM A COMFORTABLE ROOM IN THE DUNGEON WHERE HE CAN WORK UNDISTURBED TO BRING THE RECORDS UP TO DATE, CORRECTLY."*

"MY LORDS, ON MY LAST VISIT WE WERE AT WAR. THEN YOU WERE ALL RESPECTED MERCHANTS, BANKERS, TRADERS, AND WE DO NOT FORGET THE CONTRIBUTIONS YOU MADE TO OUR VICTORY. SINCE THEN PROSPERITY HAS BRED GREED AND THE HUNGER FOR POWER THAT WEALTH CAN BRING."

ONE BY ONE SHE FEEDS THE MYSTERIOUS NOTES TO THE FLAMES, ALL EXCEPT THE LAST. HERE SHE FROWNS AND HER EYES SEARCH THE FACES OF THE COUNCIL. *"THIS ONE WE SHALL KEEP,"* AND IT IS FOLDED NEATLY AND TUCKED IN HER BOSOM. *"THE COUNCIL IS DISMISSED."*

VAL SHAKES HIS HEAD IN WONDER. *"I WATCHED YOU FROM THE GALLERY AS YOU REDUCED THOSE POMPOUS, STERN COUNCILORS TO NAUGHTY SCHOOLBOYS. THERE WILL BE MANY RESIGNATIONS AMONG THOSE WHO HAVE A GUILTY CONSCIENCE BECAUSE OF THE SHEET YOU DID NOT BURN. WHAT DOES IT CONTAIN?"*
AN ELFIN GRIN SETS THE DIMPLES DANCING AS SHE TAKES FROM HER BOSOM.....A BLANK PAPER!

NEXT WEEK— **Enter Ortho Bey**

6-2

1634

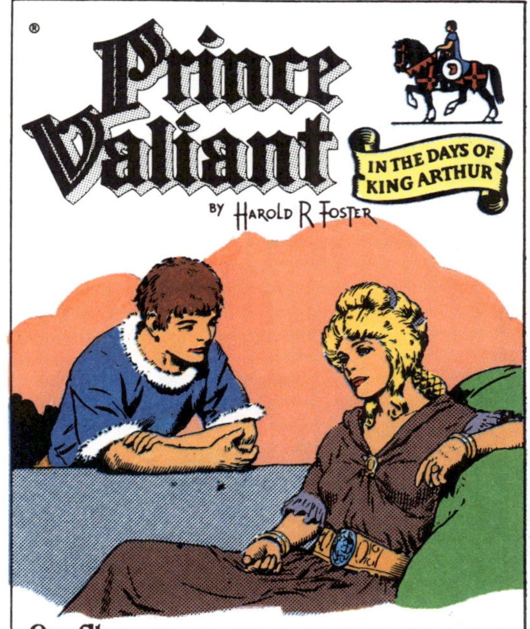

Our Story: PRINCE ARN COMPLIMENTS HIS MOTHER ON THE WAY SHE HAS TIDIED UP HER KINGDOM. "BUT THE WORK HAS JUST BEGUN," SHE SIGHS. "OUR PROSPERITY IS STILL THE ENVY OF OUR NEIGHBORS AND WE ARE UNPROTECTED."

"EVEN NOW YOUR FATHER IS BUSY WITH THE SHIP BUILDERS, CONVERTING THE ORNATE TUBS INTO TRIM FIGHTING SHIPS...

...WHILE SIR GAWAIN IS TRAINING THE ARMY. SOLDIERS ACCUSTOMED TO STANDING GUARD AT SOCIAL FUNCTIONS AND MARCHING IN PARADES FIND IT RATHER HARD WHEN THEY MUST TRAIN IN FULL ARMOR LIKE WARRIORS."

"FOR DANGER LURKS IN LYCIA WHERE THE RUTHLESS ORTHO BEY HARRIES HIS NEIGHBORS BY LAND AND SEA. OUR SPIES REPORT THAT HE IS BUILDING MANY SHIPS IN SECRET AND WE FEAR HIS GREEDY EYES ARE LOOKING TOWARD THE MISTY ISLES."

MANY HAVE RESIGNED FROM THE COUNCIL AND THEIR PLACES FILLED BY TRUSTED MEN WHO KNOW MORE OF GOVERNMENT. THEY ADVISE SENDING A MISSION TO ESTABLISH A FAVORABLE TRADE AGREEMENT WITH LYCIA AND, WHILE THERE, TO FIND OUT, IF POSSIBLE, WHAT THE BEY IS UP TO.

"MOTHER, I WISH TO GO ON THIS MISSION. IF ORTHO BEY PLANS MISCHIEF TO YOUR KINGDOM HE WILL REGARD YOUR ENVOY WITH SUSPICION. BUT WHO WOULD SUSPECT A SPOILED BOY, A PAMPERED PRINCE WHO STILL PLAYS WITH TOYS?"

VAL AND ALETA EXCHANGE GLANCES. ARN SIMPERS CHILDISHLY......

...AND SO WHEN THE SHIP SAILS PRINCE ARN IS ON IT....WITH A BOX OF TOYS.

NEXT WEEK— Suspicion

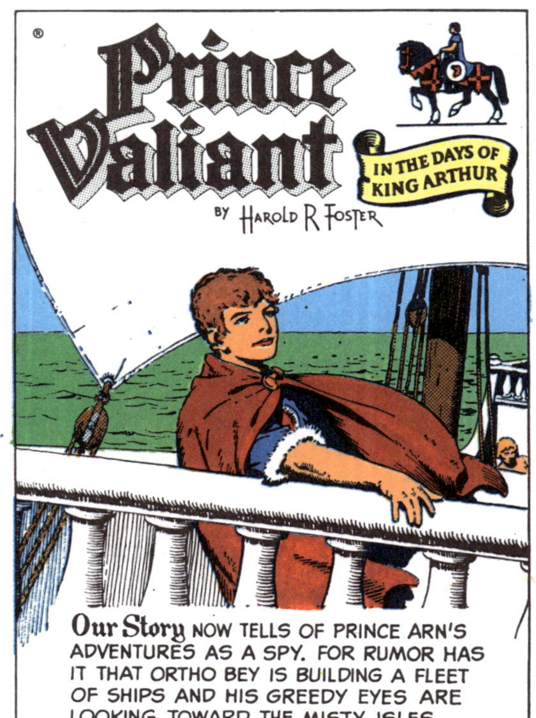

Our Story NOW TELLS OF PRINCE ARN'S ADVENTURES AS A SPY. FOR RUMOR HAS IT THAT ORTHO BEY IS BUILDING A FLEET OF SHIPS AND HIS GREEDY EYES ARE LOOKING TOWARD THE MISTY ISLES.

ON THE PRETEXT OF FORMING A TRADE AGREEMENT WITH THE BEY, QUEEN ALETA SENDS HER TRUSTED SPIES TO FIND OUT IF HER KINGDOM IS THREATENED.

THEY SAIL UP THE COAST OF LYCIA AND COME TO KAHMAR, THE WALLED CITY OF THE BEY. THE SHOALS AND ROCKS THAT GUARD THE HARBOR ENTRANCE ARE A BETTER DEFENSE THAN THE HIGH BATTLEMENTS.

IN THE HARBOR ARE MANY SHIPS, NOT CUMBERSOME MERCHANT VESSELS BUT TRIM AND SWIFT-LOOKING CRAFT THAT MIGHT WELL SUIT A CORSAIR.

AND THE SAILORS IN THE PORT GO FULLY ARMED AND CARRY THEIR WEAPONS WITH THE EASE OF LONG FAMILIARITY, AND THEIR FIERCE LOOKS PROCLAIM THEM PIRATES. SO, KAHMAR IS THE PORT FROM WHICH THE CORSAIRS PREY ON SHIPPING!

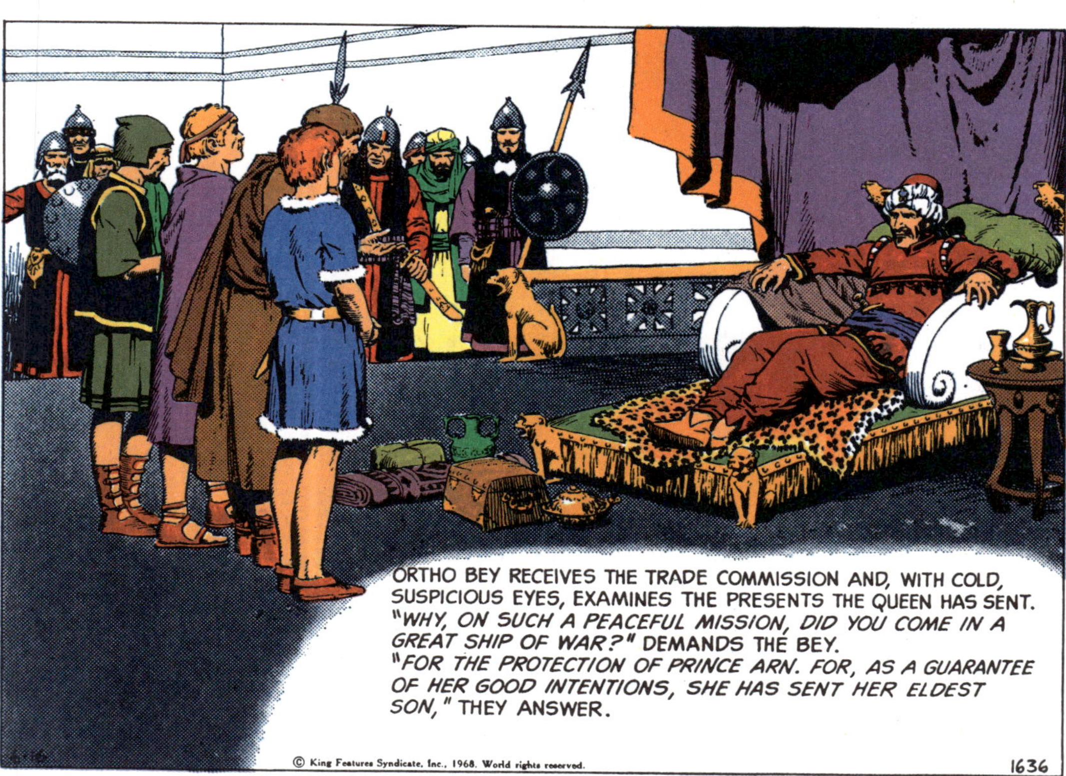

ORTHO BEY RECEIVES THE TRADE COMMISSION AND, WITH COLD, SUSPICIOUS EYES, EXAMINES THE PRESENTS THE QUEEN HAS SENT. "WHY, ON SUCH A PEACEFUL MISSION, DID YOU COME IN A GREAT SHIP OF WAR?" DEMANDS THE BEY.
"FOR THE PROTECTION OF PRINCE ARN. FOR, AS A GUARANTEE OF HER GOOD INTENTIONS, SHE HAS SENT HER ELDEST SON," THEY ANSWER.

1636

WHEN THEY HAVE GONE THE BEY GIVES ORDERS: "HAVE THEM WATCHED NIGHT AND DAY. AND YOU, OMAR, MAKE FRIENDS WITH THE PRINCE, GAIN HIS CONFIDENCE. HIS CHILDISH PRATTLE MAY REVEAL SOMETHING."
NEXT WEEK – Omar, the Watchdog

Our Story: EARLY NEXT MORNING OMAR COMES ABOARD. "THE BEY SENDS GREETINGS AND HAS GIVEN ME THE GREAT HONOR OF SHOWING YOU THE WONDERS OF OUR CITY. WHAT WOULD YOU LIKE TO SEE?"

"I LOVE SHIPS. LOOK HOW GRACEFULLY THEY SIT IN THE WATER, EAGER TO BE OFF TO SEA AND VISIT STRANGE FAR LANDS AND TRADE FOR WONDROUS CARGOES!" (OMAR MUTTERS TO HIMSELF, "MUST I LISTEN TO THIS KIND OF CHILDISH PRATTLE ALL DAY?")

"THIS IS OUR SHIPYARD, ARN. IT USED TO BE A BUSY PLACE, BUT NOW THERE IS BUT ONE HALF-FINISHED BOAT. IT IS SAD THAT OUR FLEET IS SO DIMINISHED."

"SEE HOW CLUMSY OUR SHIPBUILDERS ARE. THEY WASTE MORE TIMBER THAN THEY USE." AND OMAR LOOKS AT ARN TO SEE IF HE ACCEPTS THIS BIT OF MISINFORMATION, BUT ARN SEEMS TO PAY LITTLE ATTENTION. ("SPOILED, STUPID BRAT," WHISPERS OMAR TO HIMSELF.)

BUT THAT NIGHT IT WOULD APPEAR THAT ARN HAS HEARD AND SEEN A GREAT DEAL. "ORTHO BEY BUILDS NO VESSELS IN THE SHIPYARD, BUT MANY MEN ARE HEWING SHIP'S TIMBERS, AND A RED-AND-BLACK BOAT IS BEING LOADED WITH SHAPED RIBS AND PLANKING, MASTS AND SPARS."

"I SUSPECT THE BEY IS BUILDING HIS FLEET IN SOME HARBOR DOWN THE COAST. I WILL TRY TO OBSERVE WHERE THE RED-AND-BLACK VESSEL GOES."

"MASTER, WE HAVE KEPT WATCH OVER THE MISSION FROM THE MISTY ISLES DAY AND NIGHT. THEY SEEK NO INFORMATION AND ASK NO QUESTIONS EXCEPT ABOUT TRADE." "KEEP UP THE WATCH," ORDERS THE BEY. "AND WHAT OF THE BOY?" "PAH!" ANSWERS OMAR, "HAREM-BRED, WOMAN-RAISED, INTERESTED ONLY IN TOYS."

NEXT WEEK— The Red-and-Black Ship.

6-23
© King Features Syndicate, Inc., 1968. World rights reserved.
1637

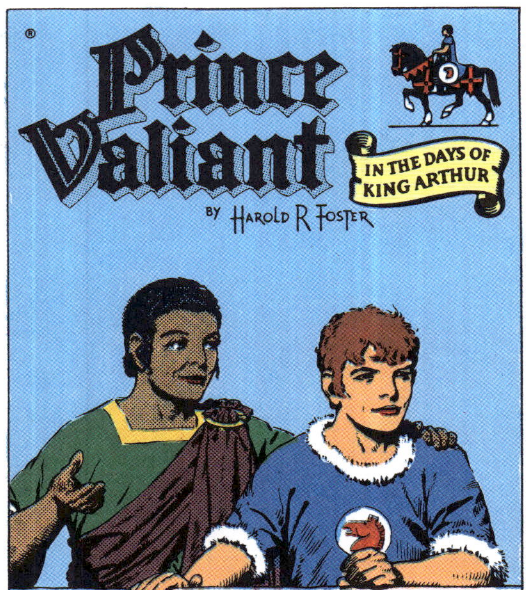

Our Story: WITH THE DAWN COMES OMAR: "WHAT SHALL WE DO THIS FINE DAY, YOUNG FRIEND?" HE EXCLAIMS WITH FALSE HEARTINESS. ARN IS WATCHING THE RED-AND-BLACK SHIP MOVING TOWARD THE HARBOR ENTRANCE WITH ITS CARGO OF SHIP'S TIMBERS....

......"LET'S GO UP INTO THE HILLS BEYOND THE CITY WALLS," SAYS ARN. THIS SUITS OMAR FOR HE HAS BEEN ORDERED TO KEEP THE YOUNG PRINCE FROM LEARNING TOO MUCH. BUT FROM THIS HEIGHT ARN SEES THE SHIP ABOUT TO PASS BEHIND A JUTTING HEADLAND.

"WHAT A PRETTY BEACH. I AM GOING FOR A SWIM!" AND ARN RACES DOWN THE HILLSIDE AND PLUNGES INTO THE SEA. OMAR, DESERT BORN, HATES THE SEA AND IS FILLED WITH FEAR AS HIS YOUNG CHARGE SWIMS FAR OUT AMONG THE TOSSING WAVES.

OMAR HAS HEARD THAT THE MISTY ISLES ARE FAMED FOR THEIR SWIMMERS BUT THIS IS TOO MUCH. HE RACES UP THE BEACH TO WHERE SOME FISHERMEN ARE MENDING NETS AND OFFERS THEM A HANDFUL OF COINS TO LAUNCH THEIR BOAT.

ARN SWIMS OUT BEYOND THE HEADLAND. THE RED-AND-BLACK SHIP IS STILL SAILING UP THE COAST, BUT FROM ARN'S POSITION LOW IN THE WATER HE CAN ONLY SEE THE TOP OF ITS SAILS. SOON IT WILL BE LOST TO HIS VIEW. THEN THE BOAT ARRIVES.

"I AM MOST GRATEFUL, OMAR. I SWAM OUT TOO FAR AND MIGHT NOT HAVE MADE IT BACK," HE LIES, AND CLIMBS UPON A SEAT TO DRY IN THE SUN. NOW HE CAN SEE THE SHIP QUITE CLEARLY AS IT TURNS AT RIGHT ANGLES AND HEADS IN TOWARD LAND.

"I BELIEVE ORTHO BEY IS BUILDING MANY SHIPS, NOT HERE IN THE HARBOR SHIPYARD, BUT IN A SECRET PLACE FIVE MILES UP THE COAST," HE REPORTS.

THEN HE HAS A SMALL SKIFF PAINTED BLACK BOTH INSIDE AND OUT. "I PLAN TO GO FISHING," HE GRINS.

NEXT WEEK— Fishing for What?

6-30

Our Story: WHEN OMAR APPEARS NEXT MORNING HIS ROYAL CHARGE IS PULLING AWAY IN A SMALL BOAT.
"I AM GOING FISHING, OMAR. WILL YOU COME ALONG?" ASKS ARN. OMAR SHAKES HIS HEAD. HE FEARS THE SEA, AND THE SKIFF SEEMS TOO SMALL TO HOLD BOTH OF THEM.

BUT OMAR FOLLOWS ALONG THE SHORE, MUTTERING ANGRILY THAT HE SHOULD BE GIVEN THE TASK OF WATCHING THIS SELF-WILLED CHILD.

ON A SANDY BEACH A MILE OR MORE BEYOND THE HARBOR BREAKWATER ARN COMES ASHORE. "LOOK, OMAR, WE WILL HAVE LOBSTERS FOR DINNER." CARELESSLY HE PULLS HIS BOAT UP ON THE SAND AND HE AND OMAR WALK BACK TO THE CITY.

IN THE DARK OF A MOONLESS NIGHT, ARN, DRESSED ALL IN BLACK, LOWERS HIMSELF INTO THE HARBOR.

THE GUARDS COULD HAVE SEEN A BOAT LEAVING AND WOULD HAVE STOPPED IT, BUT ARN IS INVISIBLE AS HE SWIMS CLOSE IN THE SHADOW OF THE WALL.

A LONG SWIM BRINGS HIM TO THE BEACH WHERE HE HAS LEFT HIS SKIFF. HE LAUNCHES IT QUIETLY AND MUFFLES THE OARS WITH CLOTH.

HE PULLS UP THE COAST. THE GHOSTLY FOAM OF BREAKERS SHOWS HIM WHERE THE ROCKS AND SHOALS ARE.

THE SOUND OF HAMMERING IS HEARD. HE ROUNDS A POINT AND IN THE TWINKLING LIGHT OF MYRIAD LANTERNS SEES THE DIM OUTLINES OF MANY SHIPS AND THE MOVING FIGURES OF A HOST OF WORKERS.

NEXT WEEK — The Nymph

7-7   © King Features Syndicate, Inc., 1968. World rights reserved   1639

Our Story: BY THE TWINKLING LIGHT OF MYRIADS OF LANTERNS, SHIPWRIGHTS ARE WORKING THROUGH THE NIGHT. THE HULLS OF MANY SHIPS ARE SILHOUETTED AGAINST THE GLOW. PRINCE ARN HAS FOUND THE HIDDEN COVE WHERE ORTHO BEY IS BUILDING HIS FLEET IN SECRET.

HOURS LATER HE ARRIVES AT THE BEACH FROM WHICH HE HAD STARTED, BEING CAREFUL TO DRAW HIS BOAT UP IN THE SAME GROOVE THE KEEL HAD LEFT, SO NONE MAY KNOW THE SKIFF HAS BEEN USED.

HAMPERED BY HIS BLACK GARMENTS, THE LONG SWIM TO THE HARBOR IS A WEARY ONE, AND ARN ARRIVES BACK AT HIS SHIP IN THE GRAY OF EARLY DAWN.

"I HAVE FOUND THE SECRET SHIPYARD WHERE ORTHO BEY IS BUILDING A FLEET OF SHIPS. WORK GOES ON DAY AND NIGHT. THE HASTE AND SECRECY POINT TO A SURPRISE ATTACK, BUT ON WHOM? THE MISTY ISLES ARE RICH BUT SADLY LACKING IN SHIPS OF WAR, AND SEEM A LIKELY TARGET, BUT WE MUST BE SURE."

WITH THE SUN COMES OMAR WITH A FALSE SMILE ON HIS LIPS AND DISLIKE IN HIS EYES. HE IS HEARTILY SICK OF BEING GUIDE, COMPANION (AND SPY) TO THE YOUNG PRINCE. AND ARN, WEARY FROM THE NIGHT'S ADVENTURE, MUST PLAY HIS PART OF A SPOILED AND WILLFUL CHILD. KNOWING HOW OMAR HATES THE SEA, ARN IS SURPRISED WHEN HE IS LED TO A BEAUTIFUL SANDY COVE.

"HERE YOU CAN SWIM TO YOUR HEART'S CONTENT," SAYS OMAR HEARTILY. "AS FOR ME, I WILL BE IN THE SHADE OF YONDER OLIVE GROVE. CALL ME WHEN YOU WISH."

FOR THE FIRST TIME SINCE HE CAME TO KAHMAR ARN IS ALONE.....BUT IS HE? SOMEWHERE A GIRL IS SINGING A SWEET GIRLISH SONG. HE FOLLOWS THE SOUND AND THERE, STRETCHED OUT IN THE SUN, IS THE MOST BEAUTIFUL GIRL HE HAS EVER SEEN.

NEXT WEEK— **The Siren**